Beginner's Guide to
Color Therapy

This book is gratefully dedicated to Lynne Lauren and her exceptional talents.

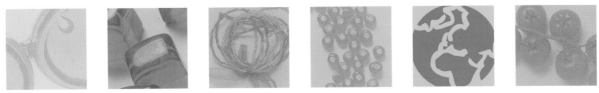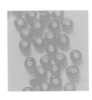

Beginner's Guide to
Color Therapy

Jonathan Dee
& Lesley Taylor

Sterling Publishing Co., Inc.
New York

Creative director: Sarah King
Editor: Lucinda Hawksley
Project editor: Sally MacEachern
Designer: Axis Design Editions

Library of Congress Cataloging-in-Publication Data Available

10   9   8   7   6   5   4   3   2   1

Published in 2003 by Sterling Publishing Co., Inc.
387 Park Avenue South, New York, N.Y. 10016

This book was designed and produced by
D&S Books Ltd
Kerswell, Parkham Ash
Bideford, Devon, EX39 5PR

© 2002 D&S Books Ltd

Distributed in Canada by Sterling Publishing
c/o Canadian Manda Group,
One Atlantic Avenue, Suite 105
Toronto, Ontario, Canada M6K 3E7

Every effort has been made to ensure that all the information in this book is accurate.
however, due to differing conditions, tools, and individual skills, the publisher cannot
be responsible for any injuries, losses, and other damages which may result from the
use of the information in this book.

Printed in China

Sterling ISBN 1-4027-1011-9

Contents

Color is found in every part of our lives. It enhances our mood, lifts our spirits, affects our emotions and behavior, and influences the way we see ourselves and others. Colors affect our way of thinking, both our conscious and subconscious attitudes. To use color effectively, one first needs to understand the psychological impact that color can create on our choice of decor, dress, work, and environment. If we understand these aspects, color can be used to enhance our lives in a positive way.

● *Color is all around us.*

Red

Red is dynamic, energizing, and physically stimulating. It also has the greatest emotional impact of any color. The emotions evoked by red range from passion, love, and lust to anger, rage, and murder. Red is both warm and safe and bold and dangerous. It is considered a good morale-booster and is seen as a valuable aid to self-assertiveness.

● *Red can symbolize passion and strong anger.*

● *Children are generally attracted to red items.*

Red is associated with grandeur in decor: take as an example Victorian theaters, whose interiors were decked with plush, red velvet. In your own home, reds are good for decorating the lounge or living room as they create a feeling of warmth and cosiness. However, too much red can also prove unsettling: given a choice of color, young children are invariably attracted to red, although tests have proved that they become agitated and irritable in a red-painted classroom.

In Eastern symbolism, red was considered to be the color of good fortune long before the Communist takeover of the 1940s. Likewise, in Russia, red was symbolic of national pride long before it became the symbol of revolution. The central plaza in Moscow has been known as Red Square since the time of Ivan the Terrible in the 16th century.

● *Pink represents softness and femininity.*

Red's dynamic intensity dramatically alters when it is mixed with white, becoming pink. The red softens, becomes gentle, and is more specifically associated with a gender, being claimed as feminine. Pink is also associated with flowers, especially the rose (the word *rose* means "pink" in the French language). Pink has no real negative connotation: if you're in the pink, everything in life is rosy.

● *Red is associated with luxury and grandeur.*

● *Pink has an association with skin, often evoking the parenting instinct.*

Pink

Many pinks are also considered sexy, associated as they can be with the color of flesh. This association with skin also creates an unconscious evocation of the parenting instinct. However, if pink is overused or used distastefully, it can have a physically weakening effect.

Pink is a popular color for bedroom decor and will encourage physical relaxation and sleep. However, it has to be balanced with either blue or green or you may find that you still feel sleepy when you wake up, instead of feeling refreshed.

● *Pink is a relaxing bedroom color, and is particularly refreshing when mixed with green or blue.*

Blue

Blue is associated with the sky and the seas, and the calming vastness of both. Blue is also associated with the intellect and with healing. It is considered the world's most popular color in fashion and decor. Wearing lighter blue tones induces gentleness and a reflective mood; wearing darker blue has come to denote efficiency and authority, as in the widespread use of deep blue and navy in the uniforms of police, firefighters, and pilots. However, denim, which can be all shades of blue, from faded white-blue to deep indigo, is the color of young fashion and has radically changed many concepts of the color blue.

● *Blue is associated with the sky.*

On an unconscious level, blue instills calm, logical thought in a stressful world. It is the peacemaker of colors: soothing, orderly, and cool. Blue encourages self-centering and mental effort. In its negative form it is used to denote sadness and depression, often called "the blues."

● *Denim in all sorts of shades is always associated with young fashion.*

● *Blue is associated with the vastness of the sea.*

● *Yellow is associated with the fall.*

Yellow

Yellow has the highest reflectivity of all colors. It is a mind-stimulating color focusing on the ego, creativity, and optimism. Light, bright, bold, and extrovert, yellow is the color of the sun and the richness of gold. A fundamental color of spring and fall, yellow is associated with natural attractiveness, both in nature and in more artificial fashions, such as the trend for platinum-blonde hair.

Yellow will brighten and lift a room, though shades of yellow should be chosen carefully for those working with emotionally fragile people, such as counselors or social workers, as it is a highly stimulating color of both good and bad emotions.

● *Yellow is the color of spring.*

Green

Green can help to promote perfect balance within our psychological makeup. It is the most restful color to the eye as it requires no retinal adjustment to focus on it. Green is believed to evoke a state of positive mental attitude and, being the color of natural foliage, makes us feel stable and secure. Emerald greens are both balancing and uplifting, as are more yellowish greens. The word "green" has come to be synonymous with the environment and selflessness.

● *Green can be restful, balancing, and uplifting.*

It should be remembered, however, that green has a dual function as it also signifies the opposite of balance—the dangerous emotions of jealousy and envy. This duality is also seen in the association of green with health: we eat green, leafy vegetables for health, yet conventionally prescribed medicines are rarely, if ever, green in color because of an old association with poison. Psychologically, humans both embrace green and retract from it. That is why, if you are choosing to decorate with greens, you should take great care when choosing the shade, as greens can give out such mixed messages.

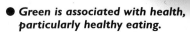

● *Green is associated with health, particularly healthy eating.*

Orange

Orange has similar, though more restrained, qualities to yellow: it is considered cheerful, uplifting, extroverted, and expansive. A bridge between red and yellow, orange possesses the impact of neither. It is quite often put with yellow as a "bright" color.

Through its connections with red, orange is an enhancer of physical passion. It also evokes the secondary survival instincts of food, shelter, warmth, comfort, and security. Orange can vary widely and it is well worth being aware of the different feelings that it can convey: a muddy shade can feel irritating and cheap in fashion and can also create a sense of physical deprivation in decor; whereas a pure, rich hue will always look opulent and very sensual.

● *Orange is often paired with yellow in decor for a cheerful, yet not overstimulating, effect.*

Brown

Brown, a darkened pigment of orange, is linked to comfort and security. It is the color of the earth—a strong, practical color.

● *Brown can represent the strength and richness of the earth.*

● *A suntan is still considered desirable.*

We build our homes with brown-orange bricks, brown our food when cooking, and, despite all the current health warnings, a bronzed suntan is still instinctively associated with ruddy health. Brown also evokes a sense of luxury by association with such items as chocolate, tea, and rich coffee. Interestingly, copper and the metallic lusters tend to be more attractive to adults rather than children, suggesting that adults' reactions are actually a learned response to objects of value.

Despite the safe, earthy connotations of brown, the color also has negative implications. Over the centuries, painters have used brown to convey sadness in their work. In the French language, *brun* means melancholy, dull, and gloomy, and in modern-day speech the expression "browned off" means to be unhappy.

● *The color of lavender is one of the more relaxing shades of violet and purple.*

Violet and Purple

Red and blue are wide apart on the color spectrum and evoke opposite traits physically, emotionally, and symbolically. However, when mixed together to form violet, they become associated with spirituality. For centuries purples have been associated with royalty and with religion as purple was the most expensive dye to produce. Psychologically, purples and violets are believed to promote peaceful mental reflection and to be indicative of high self-esteem.

● *Gray is associated with industrialization.*

Gray

Gray is the only totally neutral color and is used in fashion as a "nonstatement." Gray is often considered negative and associated with sadness, such as gray skies, industrialization, and uncertain shadows, or with insipidness. More positively, gray denotes wisdom and the intellect —being associated with the "gray matter" of the brain—although gray can also be suggestive of confusion and lack of distinction, for instance, in cases where there is said to be no "black and white," only shades of gray.

Black

How the color black is perceived depends largely on what aspect of life it is viewed from and to which culture it is related. In a spiritual sense, black is regarded as a psychically protective color; in the world of fashion it represents cool, sophisticated elegance; and with cars and modern interior decor it gives an air of sleek luxury.

● *Black can be associated with death and mourning.*

Yet in most other Western associations the color black is thought to be negative, as it is associated so prominently with death and the funereal color of mourning. It is also linked to darkness, fear of the unknown, and the occult ("black magic"). In purely technical decorative terms, black is an absorber of light and, as such, can promote bad moods.

● *In fashion, black can represent cool sophistication.*

White

The complete opposite to black, white evokes a psychology of cleanliness, purity, and aspiration: it is totally reflective and therefore associated with pure light. There are very few negative connotations with the color white in Western culture, though in other parts of the world it is the traditional color of death and mourning.

Negatively, however, if one's complexion "turns white," it suggests a bloodless and ghastly state of health. White can also be seen as insipid and lacking in passion. In decor it can be seen as a harsh and demanding color.

● *White is associated with purity.*

Chapter 1 Color Symbolism

Awareness of color is so basic to human beings that, throughout the ages, the tints, hues, and tones around us have developed many symbolic associations. This habit of imbuing color with attributes and overtones has led to a wealth of meaning. Red is the color of anger and passion, green can be unlucky, yellow denotes a coward, and so on. The following pages reveal the secrets of the symbolism of the spectrum.

Chapter 1 Color Symbolism

Throughout history, the symbolism of color has influenced us in the way we view aspects of life, emotional situations, the natural world, and each other. Superstitions and established folk wisdom have had a bearing on our code of dress, our decor, and our view of various sections of society. Historically, color has been used to denote class, luxury, fashion trends, health, and sexual matters.

Red

Red has been a symbol of the aristocracy and of royal attire. It was adopted for fox-hunting in England when King Henry II decreed it a royal sport. To roll out a red carpet, be it figuratively or literally, is regarded as the greatest show of respect. Revolution is symbolized by the red flag, and in China red symbolizes the South, where its most recent revolution began.

Red is often used as a symbol of sex and of the female genitalia. In Puritan times, a "scarlet woman" was branded with a scarlet letter; in later times, a red light became the symbol of prostitution.

Red was considered a good color to wear when going into battle as it equates with the heart and flesh. The use of red in traditional military uniforms had the effect of lifting the spirits, as well as providing a useful camouflage for blood.

● *Red was considered a good color for traditional military uniforms.*

Red symbolizes blood violently spilled. The expression "to be caught red-handed" originated from the offender still being stained with the victim's blood. This association with blood, however, also equates red with life itself. As such, the color has been revered by many tribal groups, who believed it to hold special magical powers.

● *Red can symbolize blood.*

Historically, alchemists considered red as the key to all knowledge. It was believed to be the sign that one had reached the final attainment of the philosopher's stone —which gave the possessor the ability to change base metal into gold.

● *Red was a sign that one had succeeded in changing base metal into gold.*

● *Pink is symbolic of femininity.*

Pink

Pink symbolizes the best: that one is at the height or the peak of things. This is expressed in the common sayings "in the pink" or "everything is rosy," which is symbolic of health and abundance. Pink is also symbolic of femininity and female babies.

Blue

Although, in Britain, traditional colors for babies are "pink for a girl and blue for a boy," in France, it is traditional to dress girls in the color of the Virgin Mary's blue cloak. As its name suggests, royal blue is representative of royalty, signifying the Virgin Mother's status as the queen of heaven.

Blue has been symbolic of religious hierarchy since the times of ancient Greece and Rome, when Zeus and Jupiter were worshiped in blue pantheons. The color has also been adopted as a symbol of the Union Army during the American Civil War and in police and military forces around the world.

Blue has been symbolic of the top echelons in British society since 1348, when King Edward III placed a blue garter (originally worn by the countess of Salisbury) around his knee and created the highest order of knighthood in England. It led to blue being applied to

● *Blue is the color of many uniforms.*

the greatest honors in the land. For instance, blue is the color of the archbishopric of Canterbury, called the "blue ribbon" of the Church. The most prestigious horse race, the Derby, is also symbolized by a blue ribbon. To be described as having "blue blood" came to mean being aristocratic or a member of royalty.

Blue also has its more sleazy or negative side. A "blue gown" became a term commonly used to describe a prostitute, because imprisoned prostitutes were forced to wear blue dresses to denote their crime. "Blue movies" and "blue humor" indicate pornography, and blue was traditionally the color used to describe a drunk. Blue also represents sadness, "to have the blues"; hence the soulful, emotionally compelling nature of "blues" music.

● *We often talk about "the blues," meaning sadness.*

Yellow

Yellow is the natural symbol of enlightenment and a color associated with positivity. However, it also has many negative connotations.

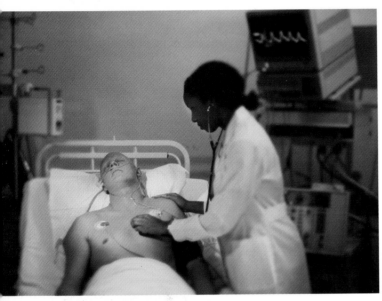

● *Yellow has signified illness for centuries.*

From medieval times, yellow has signified illness; it has also long been associated with cowardice. In recent centuries, the color became linked with scandalous (or "damaging," as the authorities believed) literature. An American cartoon paper called *The Yellow Kid* led to the development of the term "yellow press" as a description of a vulgar sensational newspaper; in 19th-century Britain, "yellow novels" were pornographic novels in characteristic yellow covers, usually imported illegally.

Green

Traditionally, green was worn at weddings as a symbol of fertility (though some wedding lore also describes green as an unlucky color for weddings). In Egyptian mythology, green represented Osiris, a powerful god associated both with life-giving vegetation and with death.

Although being described as "green" now suggests environmental awareness, for many centuries the term has also been used in a derogatory fashion to suggest that someone is inexperienced or naïve.

● *Green is associated with life-giving vegetation.*

Orange

Orange is symbolically connected with sexual connotations: during the Restoration of 1660 in England, it was slang for the female genitalia. The color orange was widely used by artists of this period and can be found in paintings portraying erotic symbolism. In Western wedding tradition, brides wear orange blossom as a symbol of fertility.

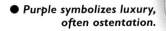

● *Purple symbolizes luxury, often ostentation.*

Violet and Purple

Purple denotes luxury and is used by royalty. Ecclesiastically, purple represents the mystery of Christ's passion and is symbolic of Easter, particularly Ash Wednesday and Holy Saturday. It can also be regarded, however, as ostentatious, being the color of wine and decadent living.

Violet symbolically relates to sensuality—a "shrinking violet" was a term used to describe a shy, reluctant, or unconfident young woman. Spiritually, violet is the symbolic color of illumination.

● *Purple can represent the decadence of rich wine.*

● *Gray can symbolize spent fuel.*

Gray

Gray is the symbolic color of the aftermath, of dust and cobwebs, of spent fuel, and of ash. It symbolizes foggy, unclear thinking and confusion.

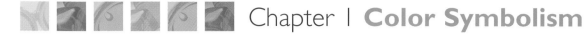

● *White is popular for brides as it represents innocence and purity.*

Black and White

In symbolism, black and white represent the good and bad, the light and the dark. White has symbolically stood for innocence and sexual purity, hence the tradition of brides wearing white to symbolize their virginity. Artists often used white, for instance, white flowers or white birds, to symbolize

the purity of a figure. Traditionally, white doves are used in art and literature to symbolize peace. White, because of its association with sunlight, is considered a symbol of holiness and of divine light.

● *White flowers often symbolize purity.*

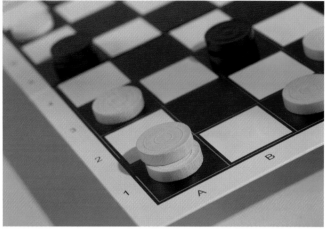

● *Despite their separate connotations, black and white are often linked together.*

Black is associated with the occult and the "black arts," a concept and religion frightening to Christian minds (as most of Western Europe was in recent centuries). The Western tradition of using the word "black" to represent negativity stems back to the times of the Crusades, when white Christian knights fought black Muslim warriors, leading to vicious racism, religious genocide, and distrust in Europe of all things "black."

In traditional English phraseology, the "black sheep of the family" is the scandalous relation, an embarrassment to the rest of the family. Black is linked with crime and ignominy in such expressions as "blackmail," "blacklisted," or "blackballed." (This latter relates to an ancient voting practice where voters were given a white and a black ball to place in the voting pot; "yes" was indicated by using the white ball, "no" by using the black ball.)

However, black also has many good connotations, especially in non-Western cultures, where white represents the same things that black suggests elsewhere. In Western cultures, black often represents tremendous strength, mystery, and a power that can be used for either good or evil.

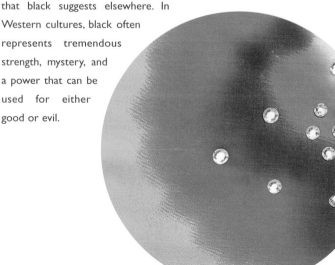

Chapter 2 **Use of Color**

Bearing in mind that color is overloaded with symbolism, its practical use in decor and dress sense has always been very important. The ancient Oriental art of Feng Shui has strict guidelines on beneficial colors and their respective elements and directions. The human electromagnetic field or aura reveals inner nature by means of color, while the energy centers, or chakras, are each strongly identified with their own particular hue. Color has its place in astrology, too, as symbolized by the zodiacal signs and their related gems and flowers.

Colour and Feng Shui

The electromagnetic energy of *chi*, sometimes translated as "the breath of life," permeates everything in the universe and is qualified as yin or yang. Black and white symbolize these two opposing forces. The white is the warm, masculine yang that contrasts with black: the cold, feminine yin.

The Four Celestial Animals

In Feng Shui philosophy, the four celestial animals, the dragon, tiger, turtle, and phoenix, are linked to the four directions, North, South, East, and West. Each of these animals has at least one color associated with it. They also represent landscape formations, as well as possessing philosophical and psychological symbolism.

The dragon, the most potent symbol of good luck, property, and abundance, is regarded as the male symbol of yang. It is linked with the east and the season of spring.

It has green as its representative color and is often referred to as the "green dragon." However, in China, the colors green and blue are often interchangeable, so the description "azure dragon" is also acceptable.

The tiger, the strong symbol of protection, is the balancing opposite of the dragon; it is therefore seen as female, relating to yin. The tiger's compass direction is the west and its season is fall. The symbolic color of the tiger is white; it is often referred to as the "white tiger."

The turtle or tortoise represents the north and connects with support, stability, and longevity. It is linked with winter and with the color black.

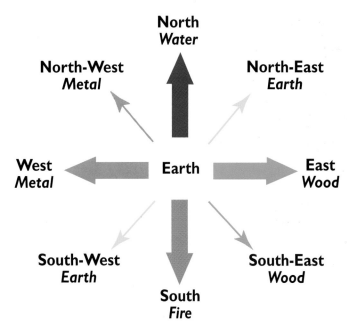

North
Water

North-West
Metal

North-East
Earth

West
Metal

Earth

East
Wood

South-West
Earth

South
Fire

South-East
Wood

The Five Elements

Each compass direction in Feng Shui is linked with an element, either water, wood, fire, earth, or metal. As there are just five elements, but eight compass directions (including South-East, South-West, North-East, and North-West), the elements wood, earth, and metal relate to more than one compass zone.

The phoenix rising from its ashes is a highly potent symbol of opportunity. Red, the color of its fire, has become symbolic of the phoenix itself. The phoenix is linked with the season of summer and connects to the south.

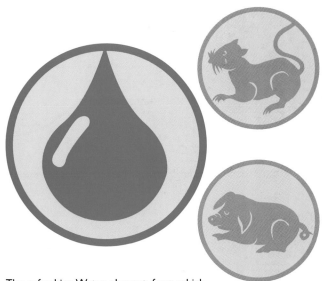

The refreshing Water element, from which all other elements emerge, has the main purpose of renewal. Water is symbolic of wealth and is linked with the North, the winter and the colors black and dark blue. These symbolically connect with the number one and the oriental zodiac signs of the rat and pig.

Wood is linked with the east and, to a lesser extent, the south-east. Symbolized by plants and flowers, it is also associated with the color green and the signs of the tiger and the rabbit.

The colors of earth, our stable, supportive, and reliable element, are brown and yellow. These belong predominantly in the South-West, but also in the North-East and in the center. The seasons linked to earth are spring and fall, and its connecting animal signs are the ox, dragon, sheep, and dog.

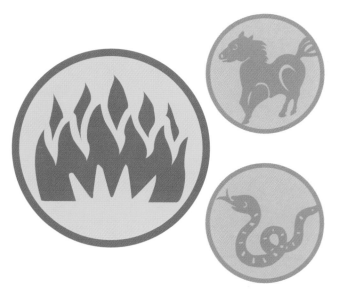

The strong element of fire is connected with the south and all reds and oranges. As a result, it is also linked to lights and candles, as well as to the signs of the horse and the snake.

The colors of metal are white, gold, and silver. It is linked with both North-West and West and with the season of fall. This element is associated with the signs of the rooster and the monkey. Metal denotes abundance and financial success, though if used in excess it can create financial aggression and greed.

Harnessing the properties of these elements in your own home is a vital part of Feng Shui. By relating the associated colors to elemental cycles and directions in the home, you can help to strengthen or mitigate the elements' effects. Symbolic objects can be used in the same way—actual objects made from the element and given the appropriate color are a good choice.

Color and the Aura

The human energy field or aura can expand up to 20 feet (6 meters) and resembles colorful, wavering outlines around the body. The outline of the aura constantly changes shape, size, and color in perfect unison with thoughts and emotions. To see the auric colors, you need to soften your eye focus and look just past the person you are viewing—think of it as adjusting your vision as you would when looking at a 3-D puzzle (or "Magic Eye") picture. Some people find that they can use their instincts and inwardly visualize the aura, taking note of the colors perceived.

Interpreting Auric Colors

Red is usually a sign of anger or anxiety, of an unforgiving nature, and also of money worries or obsessions.

Light or bright pink shows happiness, love, and compassion and can indicate a new or replenished romantic relationship. It may also indicate clairaudience (an ability to hear the voices of those who have passed on, such as spirit guides or the higher self).

Murky or dark pink can reveal immature or dishonest tendencies.

Orange shows a sociable, outgoing nature, a creative/artistic temperament, intense emotions, and a highly sexual nature. It is also seen in the aura of people currently experiencing stress induced by addictions, including overindulgence in food, drugs, or alcohol.

Pale yellow is indicative of emerging spiritual and psychic awareness. It also shows positivity, optimism, hopefulness, or excitement about new ideas.

A brilliant lemon yellow indicates a fear of losing control in a relationship, be it either business or personal. It is often seen in people struggling to keep power, prestige, and respect.

Bright gold metallic yellow shows spiritual energy awakening and inspiration.

Dark brownish yellow or gold indicates a student or a person who is undergoing training. It may also show that the person is being overly analytical, to the point where they are causing themselves stress.

A bright emerald green denotes that the subject is a healer, either a professional, such as a doctor, or a natural healer, such as a faith healer. The person with this aura could be unaware of their own abilities in this field.

An emerald-green aura around the fingertips shows "healing hands." This also shows a love-centered person.

Murky or dark green is indicative of resentment and jealousy. A person with this aura can be described as a "victim": an insecure person with low self-esteem. This person probably has little sense of personal responsibility and is very sensitive to criticism.

Pale blue shows intuition, truthfulness, and an expressive personality.

Royal blue indicates clairvoyant ability and a highly spiritual and generous nature.

Murky and dark blues tend to show a fear of speaking the truth, of self-expression, and also of the future.

Purple has very spiritual indications. If the aura is red-violet, this indicates clairaudience.

Some claim that a blue-purple aura can mean that the Archangel Michael is standing within the person's auric field.

Murky purple means that there is desperate need for love and attention.

Combined with white, purple shows truth and purity. If a woman's aura includes flashes of bright white light within the auric field, it is likely that she is, or will soon become, pregnant.

Black usually means that there are long-felt issues of forgiveness to be addressed, with negative entities lodged within the person's auric field, chakras, or body. Black can also be indicative of hurts suffered in past lives. If a woman has blackness around the ovaries, there is a probability of unreleased grief due to miscarriage or abortion.

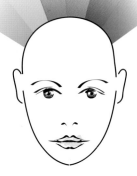

Rainbow-colored stripes protruding from the head, hands, or body indicate wonder and expectation. This feature can show a healer. It can also be indicative of a soul in its first incarnation on Earth.

 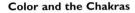 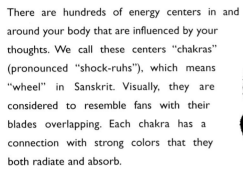

Color and the Chakras

There are hundreds of energy centers in and around your body that are influenced by your thoughts. We call these centers "chakras" (pronounced "shock-ruhs"), which means "wheel" in Sanskrit. Visually, they are considered to resemble fans with their blades overlapping. Each chakra has a connection with strong colors that they both radiate and absorb.

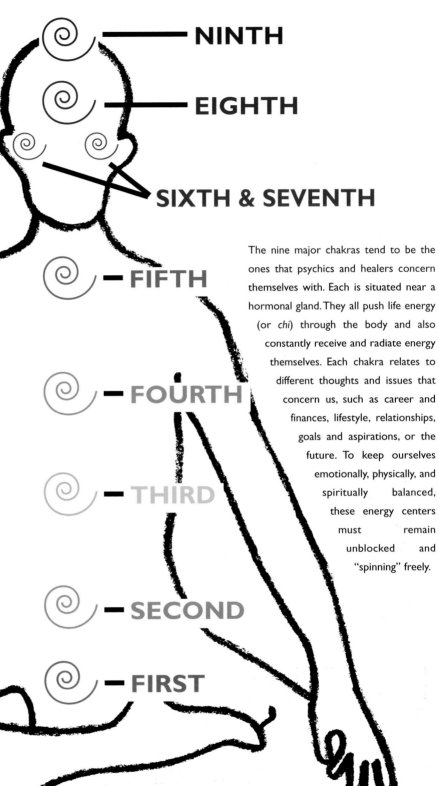

NINTH

EIGHTH

SIXTH & SEVENTH

FIFTH

FOURTH

THIRD

SECOND

FIRST

The nine major chakras tend to be the ones that psychics and healers concern themselves with. Each is situated near a hormonal gland. They all push life energy (or *chi*) through the body and also constantly receive and radiate energy themselves. Each chakra relates to different thoughts and issues that concern us, such as career and finances, lifestyle, relationships, goals and aspirations, or the future. To keep ourselves emotionally, physically, and spiritually balanced, these energy centers must remain unblocked and "spinning" freely.

If you aim for love and harmony within your life, the chakras should function correctly, providing you with energy, optimism, and drive. If you hold on to fear, bitterness, jealousy, or any form of negativity, then the corresponding chakra will become murky in color and will either shrink or swell. To clear blocked chakras usually requires meditation. The locations of the major chakras are as follows.

Located at the base of your spine is the first chakra: the base or root. This spins, creating a ruby-red color, and relates to physical security, survival instincts, such as food, shelter, and warmth, and also basic material needs.

In the abdomen is found the sacral center, 3 to 4 inches (8 to 10 centimeters) below the solar plexus. It spins slightly faster than the root chakra, appearing as a brilliant orange. This chakra connects to physical desires and emotions. It deals with physical pleasures, sex, food, and thrill-seeking. It is also associated with addictions and bodily habits, such as weight gain, health, exercise, sleep, and physical appearance.

The solar-plexus or third major chakra is found just above the navel and spins faster than the sacral chakra. This chakra is affected by thought and emotion and vibrates a pure yellow.

Power and control are centered here: control over oneself, as well as over others.

The fourth, heart, chakra deals with love and the realization of "oneness." The heart is the first of the upper chakras, and its spin is medium to fast; it resonates with the color emerald green, and also pink. The heart chakra is affected by thoughts and feelings concerning all relationships: with family, lovers, friends, colleagues, employers, teachers, peers, and strangers.

Love of all kinds—romantic, platonic, and divine, as well as love of the higher self—are centered in the heart chakra. This major chakra also deals with relationship obsessions, codependency, and negative relationship addictions, forgiveness, or lack of forgiveness. This chakra is fundamental to the development of clairsentience, or "clear feeling."

The fifth chakra, the throat chakra, is found just in front of the Adam's apple. It spins rapidly and is colored sky blue. This chakra relates to communication and speaking the truth—to yourself, as well as others. It is concerned with creative projects, such as art, singing, writing, channeling, and teaching.

The sixth and seventh chakras are inside the head, just above each ear. Their colors are maroon or red-violet. The ear chakras relate not only to divine communication and clairaudience, but also to what is heard and what has been heard, including personal phrases (usually repeated), verbal abuse, the energy of music, and environmental noises.

The chakras should be regularly cleansed to ensure that they function properly and to keep their colors bright, thus maintaining physical, emotional, and mental balance.

The eighth major chakra is known as the "third eye." It is oval in shape and is found between the physical eyes. It is called the third eye because it has an eye in the center radiating a deep indigo blue. The third eye is turned inward, facing your identity; it is the eye of your higher self. This chakra records everything that you feel, think, and do. It is believed that one watches a playback of this "life movie" when one passes on to a higher plane.

The third eye deals with how you relate to your future, as well as to the past, including past lives. It is also concerned with your beliefs about the spirit world, as well as your fear or desire to see angels or apparitions. A clear, unblocked third eye will link you strongly to your higher self.

The crown, the ninth and final chakra, lies just inside the top of the head and resembles a ceiling fan that is a rich, deep, royal purple. This is the receiving center and is concerned with claircognizance or "clear knowing": the ability to receive information and ideas from the collective unconscious or the divine mind. This chakra is often very active in creative people who can pick up inspiration from the cosmos. This chakra is related to religion or spirituality and our relationship to God and divine guidance. This chakra deals with spiritual trust, when we believe that we receive information from the etheric plane without knowing "how" we know.

Color relates strongly to astrological sun signs. It filters through from the symbolism of each zodiacal sign to its relating gemstones, flowers, and metals. The colors associated with the signs represent their personality inclinations, as well as mood and mental makeup. Areas of the body are also linked to each sign, and thereby also to a specific color.

Aries

Aries is represented by bright red, connecting the fire sign to its ruling planet, Mars, the dynamic god of war, blood, and aggression. Red is also the color of Tuesday, or "Mars' Day," and covers the areas of the Aries body, such as the head and eyes, which are prone to weakness. The lucky number for Aries is one, and the lucky gems are bloodstone and diamond. The lucky flower of this sign is honeysuckle, while its metal is iron.

● *Diamond.*

Taurus

Taurus is linked to green and pink and its symbol, the bull, is representative of strength, endurance, and sexuality. Natural greens are strongly linked here because Taurus is the first of the earth signs. Taurus is ruled by the planet Venus, hence it is associated with love and with pink, the color of love and emotion. This sign's weak body areas include the lower jaw, throat, thyroid gland, and neck. Taurus's best day is Friday (traditionally the day of the goddess Venus after whom the planet was named). The lucky number of Taurus is two, and the flowers are rose, poppy, violet, clover, and foxglove. The gemstones of this sign are topaz, sapphire, and emerald. Its metal is copper.

● *Red rose.*

Gemini

Gemini is associated with yellow, the color of thought and mental activity; yellow is believed to have a dual nature, symbolized by the Gemini twins. The sign's ruling planet is Mercury, and Wednesday is likely to be the best day of the week for mental energy. The vulnerable areas for Geminis are the upper respiratory system, the arms, and shoulders. The lucky number is three, and the flowers are lily of the valley, orchid, lavender, and gladiolus. Gemini's connecting metal is mercury. The lucky stone is agate.

● *Orchid.*

Chapter 2 **Color in Astrology**

Cancer

The moon is the planet that governs Cancer, and this orb also governs the feminine principle, travel, and the sea. The parts of the body connected to this sign are the lungs, breasts, and stomach. Cancer's best day is Monday, and its representative colors are white, silver, and pearl; as such, its lucky gems are pearl and mother of pearl. Cancer's flowers are the lotus, wild flowers, and acanthus; the lucky number is four, and its metal is silver.

● **Pearls.**

Leo

Leo's ruling planet is the sun, naturally linking it with the colors gold, yellow, orange, and cream. This zodiacal sign is linked with the Roman god Apollo, who rules music, poetry, prophecy, reason, and light. Leo's best day is Sunday, and the most vulnerable areas of the body are likely to be the heart, arteries, and circulation. The lucky gems are ruby, diamond, sardonyx, and tiger's eye, and the fortunate flowers are sunflower, marigold, nasturtium, and cyclamen. Leo's lucky number is five, and its associated metal is gold.

● **Tiger's eye.**

Virgo

Virgo has navy blue, muted greens, and gray as its colors. Virgo is governed by the planet Mercury—its special metal is also mercury. Wednesday is the day associated with Virgo, and potentially troublesome parts of the body to watch include the bowels, skin, and the nervous system. Fortunate gems are diamond, peridot (chrysolite), and sardonyx; the lucky number for Virgo is six, and its connected flowers are lily, narcissus, cornflower, and snowdrop.

● **Lily.**

Libra

Libra, the sign of balance, is ruled by Venus and has as its representative colors sky blue, leaf green, and pink. The best day for Librans is Friday, and the parts of the body to watch out for are the kidneys, bladder, and lower spine. The lucky gems are sapphire, emerald, and jade. The lucky number is seven, and its connected flowers include all types of roses.

● *Pink rose.*

Scorpio

The deeply complex sign of Scorpio is governed by Pluto. The sign is associated with the colors dark red and dark purple. The delicate body areas are the eyes, lower stomach, sexual organs, lower spine, and blood. The most fortunate day is Tuesday, and lucky gems are jet, onyx, obsidian, and opal. The lucky number for Scorpio is eight. Its associated metal is iron, and its plants include cacti and any thorny bush or tree.

● *Obsidian.*

Sagittarius

Sagittarius, the Archer, is said to be the traveler of the zodiac. It is represented by deep royal blues and imperial purple. Ruled by the planet of expansion, Jupiter, the associated gems for this sign are topaz, carbuncle, and sapphire. The lucky number is nine, and vulnerable parts of the body are likely to be the hips, thighs, and leg circulation. The lucky plants and flowers are rushes, pimpernels, dandelions, and pinks. The associated metal of the sign of the archer is tin.

● *Topaz.*

Capricorn

Saturn, the planet of limitations and hard lessons, is the ruler of Capricorn, and the colors here are earthy black, gray green, and brown. Capricorn's vulnerable body areas are the bones, teeth, skin, knees, and ears. Its best day is Saturday, and the lucky gemstones include black opal, turquoise, and tourmaline. The luckiest number for this sign is ten, and the plants to look out for are ivy, thistle, pansy, and hemlock.

● *Turquoise.*

Aquarius

The ruling planet of Aquarius is the unpredictable Uranus, which behaves differently to all the others within the solar system. A slightly different color scheme of electric blue, indigo, and neon colors is therefore associated with this sign. Vulnerable areas of the body are the ankles and circulation to the extremities. The lucky gems are amethyst and lapis lazuli, and compatible metals are uranium, lead, and platinum. Its best day is Saturday, and the lucky number is eleven. Associated flowers are the buttercup, orchid, and absinth.

● *Lapis lazuli.*

Pisces

Pisces, the psychic sign, is connected to colors reminiscent of the sea: green and turquoise are prominent as they are symbolic of Neptune, the Roman god of the sea. Vulnerable parts of the body for Pisceans are the feet, the mind, and the lungs. The lucky gems are moonstone, bloodstone, and pearl. Pisces's lucky day is Thursday, and the fortunate number is twelve. Flowers in harmony with this sign are the water lily and poppy, while the associated metal is tin.

● *Bloodstone.*

The use of color with the body has therapeutic healing effects. When dealing with ailments, it can be beneficial to meditate on certain colors, to use colored lamps on certain areas of the body, and to dress using the healing color in the appropriate area (if you have a sore throat, for instance, wear a turquoise scarf—see below for more information).

Red raises blood pressure and releases adrenaline, while orange aids digestion and the metabolic system. Red is beneficial for many blood disorders, anemia, glandular fever, and also for numbness.

Yellow is beneficial for some nervous disorders, liver ailments, jaundice, schizophrenia, and diabetes.

Orange encourages joy and a positive disposition; it also boosts the metabolic system and aids digestion. Orange can help with stomach ulcers, underactive thyroid glands (blue is used if the thyroid is overactive), stiffness of joints, liver ailments, constipation, alcoholism, and kidney disease.

Green is good for heart conditions, such as angina, and chest conditions, such as bronchitis. It is also considered to be helpful to sufferers of claustrophobia.

Turquoise relieves pain and is also an anti-inflammatory. It can be good for skin problems, such as acne and dermatitis, and for insect stings and hay fever. Turquoise and blue aid pneumonia, sinusitis, and stress.

Blue is thought to reduce blood pressure and relieve throat problems, laryngitis, and tonsillitis. It is therapeutic for itching, insomnia, motion sickness, thrush, toothache, sunburn, sneezing, stammering, and scarring.

Violet is a whole-body purifier and helps to promote healthy sleep patterns.

Magenta is used to relieve migraines and headaches and can also help to relieve nausea.

Color is the most powerful tool in the interior designer's tool-box. It can be used to replicate a particular mood or regional theme, and is so potent that it can also be used to alter the perceived shape and size of a space.

● *Color is a property of light.*

To harness the full power of color when designing, you must first understand the principles of color theory. This may sound rather tedious, and even a little confusing, but I can assure you that it is a very enjoyable and enlightening process of learning. It is rewarding to discover the reason why colors work together, and it is very exciting to find that many of the things that you may have been doing instinctively when using color do, in fact, have a firm grounding in color theory.

How Does Color Work?

The modern understanding of color began in 1666, when Sir Isaac Newton proved that color is a property of light. He projected a small beam of sunlight through a prism and displayed the emerging bands of color on a white screen. The colors that appeared were red, orange, yellow, green, blue, and violet.

In 1770, scientist Moses Harris created the first color wheel to distinguish red, yellow, and blue as the three primary colors. In the early 20th century, color theory was further extended when Johannes Itten refined color classificiation by adding secondary and tertiary colors to the wheel.

To explain this modern principle, I have chosen to show you the twelve-hue color-wheel system.

All colors are derived from the three primary colors: red, yellow, and blue. These are the only colors that cannot be made up from a combination of any other colors. By mixing each of the primary colors with one other, you produce three secondary colors: orange, green, and violet.

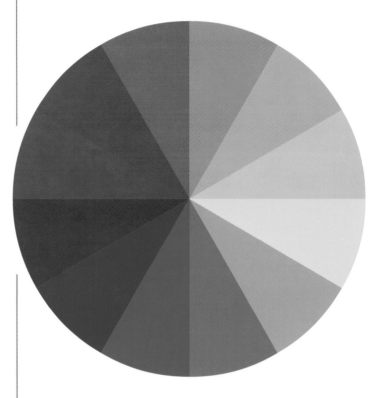

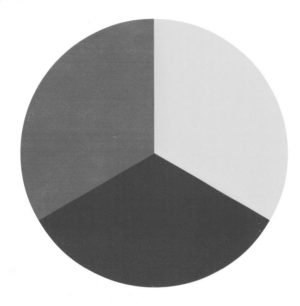

To create a twelve-hue color wheel, you take the primary and secondary colors as six of the twelve hues. The primary colors should be equally spaced around the wheel.

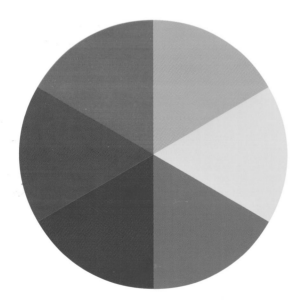

The remaining spaces are the natural home to our six intermediary, or tertiary, colors. These are produced by mixing together one primary and its neighboring secondary color. This will produce yellow-orange, red-orange, red-violet, blue-violet, blue-green, and yellow-green. When all the twelve colors are correctly positioned on the wheel, they create what is known as a "natural spectrum order."

The wheel can be further extended to a twenty-four-hue wheel. For example, between yellow and orange you could have a natural spectrum order of yellow (Y.), the primary; yellow-orange-yellow, two parts yellow to one part orange (Y.O.Y.); yellow-orange (Y.O.), your intermediary color; orange-yellow-orange, two parts orange to one part yellow (O.Y.O.); followed by orange (O.), a secondary color.

When you consider the natural order of colors on a color wheel, you will notice that the wheel can be divided further into warm and cool color spectrums.

The secondary colors, green, orange, and violet, are positioned on the wheel between their "parent colors."

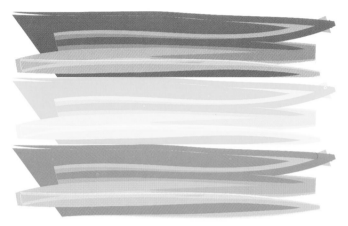

● *Warm colors.*

● *Cool colors.*

Warm and Cool Colors

Generally speaking, red, yellow, and orange are considered warm colors, and blue and green are considered cool colors. Violet is the only color that can appear to be both warm or cool, depending on the proportions of its parent colors. A hue of violet with a large proportion of blue, for instance, would appear cool, while a violet with a primarily red base would appear warm. Its appearance will also alter depending on the colors that you decide to use with it. Team violet with warm reds, and it will appear cooler than it would when combined with cool blues, for example.

Warm colors advance, so use them to create cozy color schemes. Cool colors recede, making a room look larger and therefore slightly more formal. You can harness these powers to balance badly proportioned rooms.

What is the Difference between Tone and Shade?

Colors with black and white added are known as tones.
Colors with white added are known as tints.
Colors with black added are known as shades.

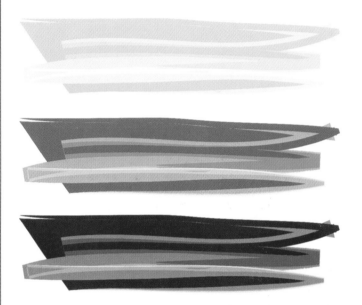

For example, red with added white creates the tint known as pink, but if black is added, it becomes a deeper burgundy shade. So in color terms, the difference between burgundy and pink, derived from the same base color, is purely a tonal variation.

Successful color-scheming is as reliant on tone as it is on color. Tone can be used to alter esthetically the proportions of a room. This is because the deeper the tone of a color, the less light can be reflected from it. Therefore, the deeper the tone, the closer the color will appear. The lighter the tone, the more reflective it becomes, making it appear farther away.

Color for Interiors: A Glossary of Terms

Here is a helpful glossary of terms that are often used when discussing the use of color in interior decorating.

Accent color – This is a color introduced to a color scheme as a highlight. It adds life and additional visual interest to a room.

Advancing colors – These colors are found on the warm side of the color wheel: reds, oranges, and yellows. They generally make a surface appear closer.

Color wheel – A tool used by designers displaying colors in their natural order. The color wheel is based on the work of Sir Isaac Newton.

Complementary – see contrasting.

Contrasting colors – Otherwise known as complementary, these are colors that lie on opposite sides of the color wheel.

Cool colors – These are colors found on one side of the color wheel: blue, green, and some violets are all cool colors.

Harmonious colors – These are combinations of color that lie next to one another on the color wheel.

Intermediate colors – These are colors found between primary and secondary colors. They are also known as tertiary.

Neutral color schemes – Decorative schemes produced by combining noncolors, such as white, black, brown, beige, and cream.

Monochromatic color schemes – Decorative schemes produced by the combination of various tones of one color.

Primary colors – Red, blue, and yellow. These are base colors that cannot be produced by mixing together any of the other colors on the color wheel.

Receding colors – Colors from the cool side of the color wheel; they can be used to make a surface appear farther away.

Shades – Colors with black added.

Tints – Colors with white added.

Warm colors – These are colors found on one side of the color wheel: red, orange, and yellow are warm colors.

Chapter 3 **Primary Colors**

The three basic colors of red, yellow, and blue are known as the primary colors. All other hues are mixtures of these three. The primaries exist independently. One cannot mix them from any other combination. As such, they represent three facets of originality. The warmth of red, the coolness of blue, and the exuberance of yellow provide the backdrop to all color theory.

Red

Red is one of the three primary colors. It is a very passionate and assertive color, associated with danger and fire. Red is hot and sometimes hard to handle.

Red is the color of life, youth, passion, and blood. It is also the predominant color associated with fire, both as a heat source and in a more spiritual sense as the energy of plasma, the atomic force that powers the universe. Red is the color of unbridled energy and of the passions that course through the blood, overwhelming the rational mind.

Red stimulates the physical senses and enhances ambitions, drives, and courage. On the physical level, being surrounded by red will increase the blood pressure and pump adrenaline into the system. Red can incite anger, sexual desire, and impulsiveness. It can be used to energize when one is exhausted, depressed, or lacking in willpower. It is also useful in banishing feelings of negativity and can be a help to shy people who wish to be more assertive. Wearing or being surrounded by red when one is overwrought or pressurized, however, can lead to outbursts of anger and aggression.

Symbolism

Red has always been associated with war gods, such as the Roman deity Mars. Interestingly, due to the reddish color of its surface dust, the planet Mars—named after the god—is often referred to as the "red planet." In

● *Red is the color of heat, passion, and energy.*

● *Redheads are often considered fiery.*

symbolism, this color is mainly associated with aggression, the arts of war, and with honorable conduct in battle. In the terminology of heraldry, red is called "gules" or "sanguine" (blood). Its appearance on a shield of honor signifies both valor and magnanimity to a fallen foe.

Red's negative or malign associations are usually connected with passion. For instance, redheads are traditionally assumed to have fiery tempers, and, of course, red is the color of blood.

Red is considered to be masculine, exultant, victorious, and ferocious. In the mythology of the Vikings, it was the color of red-bearded, hammer-wielding Thor, the thunder god. In Christian symbolism, red is the color of martyrs who have spilled their blood for the faith. In the ancient Celtic religion of the Druids, red was one of the colors of the

triple goddess, who was most often represented as the Maiden, the Mother, and the Hag. Each of these divine aspects was allocated a color suitable to her nature. The Maiden was white, the Hag was black, while the motherly aspect of the goddess was represented as red. It may be for this reason that in previous centuries brides often wore red to represent the fertility that their union would bring.

from the ashes. Red is also considered to be the color of good fortune, promoting creativity, energy, and a zest for life. Red's symbolic season is the high summer, when the sun's heat is at its greatest.

The Psychology of Red

Red represents a fiery, passionate force. Its main keyword is "action." Red is extremely positive in nature and can therefore be used to eliminate unwanted negativity in thoughts and emotions. It is particularly useful to people who are shy by nature because it encourages them to put themselves forward and to develop more self-confidence and assertive attitudes. Likewise, if one is reluctant to get started on a major project, overwhelmed by the immensity of the task ahead, wearing or surrounding oneself with red will overcome this inner barrier and allow the energies to flow.

Keywords for Red

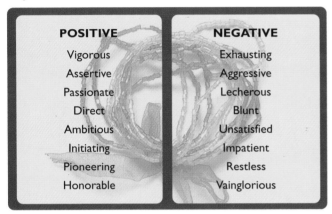

POSITIVE	NEGATIVE
Vigorous	Exhausting
Assertive	Aggressive
Passionate	Lecherous
Direct	Blunt
Ambitious	Unsatisfied
Initiating	Impatient
Pioneering	Restless
Honorable	Vainglorious

Astrology

The planet Mars is the primary association with the color red. The masculine, passionate, headstrong nature of the planet is also connected with the metal iron, the primary ingredient of weapon-makers, which, if left untreated, will quickly rust to a reddish hue. The two zodiacal signs governed by Mars are Aries and Scorpio, both of which are said to be courageous and assertive (possibly aggressive), with passionate natures.

Feng Shui

In Oriental tradition, red is associated with the element of fire. Its symbolic beast is the red bird of the south, otherwise known as the phoenix. Red therefore symbolizes rebirth because the phoenix was said to burn itself to death on a funeral pyre and then rise in glory

Red and the Body

Red prompts the release of adrenaline into the bloodstream. In astrology, the adrenal glands are said to be influenced by the "red planet," Mars. Red also promotes the "fight or flight" instinct and is thus connected with reactions of both aggression and fear.

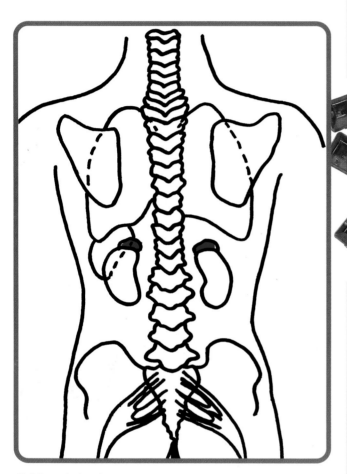

● *Adrenal glands.*

In terms of bodily ailments, being bathed in red light is said to be good for circulatory problems, irregularities of blood flow, hardening of the arteries, infertility, and anemia. However, a word of caution must be inserted here. Because red is such a powerful and often uncontrollable force, red light should not be used above the waist because of the danger of overstimulating the heart rate. If you are in any doubt, then medical advice should be sought before using chromatherapy for any pulmonary or circulatory problem. When one is feeling resentful or experiencing a simmering anger, then red should not be worn—unless you are looking for an excuse to explode. The trick with red is to make events occur your way and not to allow your passions to overrule common sense.

Red is also associated with sexual passions; it is not only connected with the sexual organs, but also with the erogenous zones and the base chakra (at the bottom of the spine). This chakra is usually colored red and symbolized by a spiritual snake, which, in Indian belief, entwines itself around the spine to carry energy to all of the other chakras.

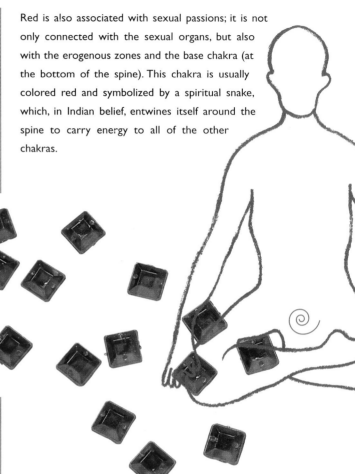

The Shades and Tints of Red
Maroon

The vibrant energies of red are somewhat subdued by this muted shade. Maroon represents a more thoughtful, considered course of action that still requires courage. Someone who favors this shade generally feels as though the odds are stacked against them, yet there are grounds for hope. With resolute actions combined with necessary caution, obstacles can be overcome.

Magenta

This shade of red is normally favored by those who find themselves in the position of arbitrating in other people's disputes. The intransigence of others is a source of irritation, yet lovers of magenta find themselves unable to express fury openly. Nevertheless, the energies of red are still present, biding their time until a resolution is found and an improvement can be made. Magenta represents the most patient aspect of this hot primary color.

Crimson

The vibrancy of crimson is representative of strength of purpose, resolute action, and utter determination to succeed; however, ruthlessness is not part of this shade's symbolism. On the contrary, a person who favors crimson will seek to avoid strife: "live and let live" is likely to be their motto. The only time when a crimson-oriented person is likely to strike out is when personal freedom is threatened.

Scarlet

Above all other tones of red, scarlet expresses an exuberant love of life; historically, the shade developed other connotations as well, especially labeling women who didn't conform to their society's sexual norms as "scarlet." A person who favors this shade has little time for convention or for boring people and realizes that one may as well cram in as much fun as one can while one is here!

Pink

Pink, a mixture of red and white, is so widely used that it has developed a symbolism of its own and is often regarded as a separate color.

Red in the Aura

The appearance of red in the aura indicates a powerful ego and a very strong will. This is a person who is governed by passions and desires, yet whose outlook is extremely farsighted. This is not a person who lives in the past: instead it is the aura of someone who is always looking for the new.

As an auric color, red signifies a time in a person's life when the most unlikely fantasies and dreams can be made to come true. The possessor of the red aura has all the energy and drive that she or he could possibly need to fulfill their aims and ambitions.

If flashes of red suddenly appear in the aura, then lust is likely to be the predominant emotion. This lust is not necessarily for sexual gratification: a new and more satisfying career may be in the offing, or a creative triumph may be indicated.

On a more negative note, red can also show deep-seated anger, making the person quick-tempered and impulsive. In this case, the color may indicate a difficult time of many trials, especially in their emotional life. A person with an aura that can be described as blood-red is usually spoiled, difficult, and very demanding.

Color Combinations

Dominant Bright Red and Yellow

This is a bad color combination to be spotted in an aura. It usually indicates that its possessor is deceiving themselves about a person who is very important to them. In this sense, the proximity of deep red and yellow may hint at infidelity within a partnership. The combination may also indicate a terrible sense of isolation, with the passion for life muted by too much introspection.

Dominant Bright Red and Dark Blue

There is a powerful urge to be dramatic in a person with this color combination present in their aura. The dark blue adds an intuitive ability to the passions of the red, usually resulting in someone who is outgoing, vibrant, excitable, and theatrical. A person with this aura usually has a tendency to exaggerate everything. However, they will never, ever be dull. If the combination of vivid red and dark blue should suddenly appear in the aura, then a flash of stunning inspiration is about to occur.

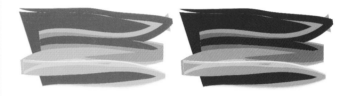

Dominant Bright Red and Crimson

The beginnings of a passionate love affair are commonly associated with the combination of bright red and crimson. This is especially true if the red in question happens to be a vibrant scarlet. To the fortunate possessor of this type of aura, the world is a wonderful place as long as he or she is close to the beloved. The only negative thing that can be said about this combination is that other people are likely to be extremely envious of this person's good luck.

Dominant Dark Red and Royal Blue

The combination of dark red and royal blue in an aura shows that this is a person who is no stranger to deep and abiding commitment. Such a person knows where they are going, has vision for the future, and is sincere in their beliefs. If this combination appears as a temporary feature in the aura, then it is time for its possessor to take on more responsibility and develop a sense of vocation.

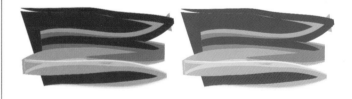

Dominant Dark Red and Pink

The combination of a dark red, such as crimson or maroon, with the soft hue of pink is indicative of falling in love. Both passion and sentiment are in tune with red and pink and provide a powerful energy. If this appears as a temporary feature in the aura, the romance will be short-lived, yet memorable. However, if this combination is a long-lasting one, then the love of one's life has been found.

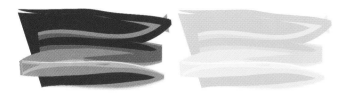

Dominant Dark Red and Light Blue

This is a combination indicative of someone who appears to be assertive and self-possessed, yet is actually rather insecure. It also points to a certain indecisiveness and a fear of taking responsibility for his or her actions. On the other hand, the possessor of such an aura is adept at taking responsibility for others and may spend a great deal of time helping people—often as a defense mechanism that effectively prevents the helper from solving his or her own problems.

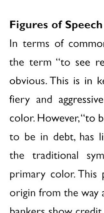
Figures of Speech

In terms of common linguistic use, the term "to see red" is the most obvious. This is in keeping with the fiery and aggressive nature of the color. However, "to be in the red," or to be in debt, has little to do with the traditional symbolism of this primary color. This phrase takes its origin from the way accountants and bankers show credit in black ink and debits in red. In the same vein, "not to have a red cent" is a more modern variation on the theme. Pointless bureaucracy is highlighted with "red tape," and, as lovers of detective stories will know, false clues are "red herrings."

● *To see "the red light" means that we should stop if we go too far.*

A "red-letter day" signifies a special occasion because in old calendars holy days were marked in red, while "painting the town red" means to embark on a noisy, and sometimes disorderly, spree. Perhaps if one goes too far, one should "see the red light" and stop rather than taking the phrase in its other sense and visiting a house of ill repute! However, if one does, there is always the possibility that one could be "caught red-handed."

The Use of Red in Decor

The color red is very passionate and assertive: in nature, it is the sign of ripened fruit, while its attractive nature is used to full effect in many courtship displays. A color associated with danger and fire, red is considered hot and sometimes hard to handle.

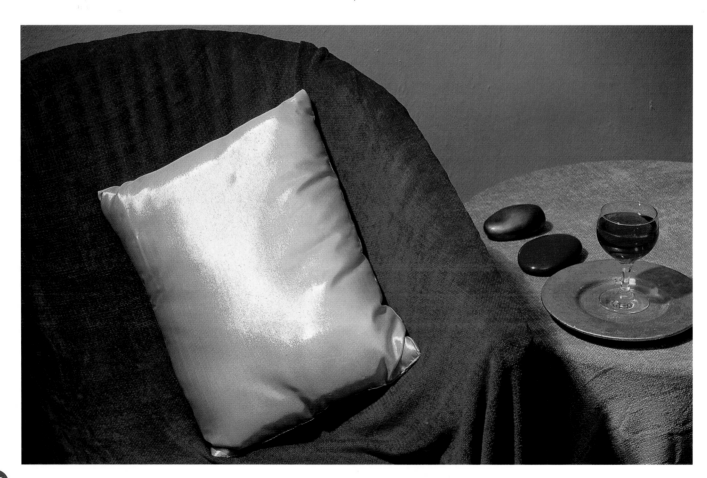

● *Red is associated with grandeur and royalty.*

One of the three primary colors, red is sited on the warm side of the color wheel. It is therefore known as an advancing color: one that reduces the perceived appearance of a space when used in decor.

For many years, bright-red pigments were very costly to produce, making red fabrics rare and expensive. A room hung with red silk drapery was seen as the height of luxury, and soon became synonymous with stately houses and royal palaces.

In decorative terms, red is also perceived as a powerful color, one that many people shy away from using within their homes. It is popular in patterned fabrics, which can successfully deliver the warmth and hospitality of red to a room's decor, but in a compact and manageable way.

● *Red is popular in patterned fabrics.*

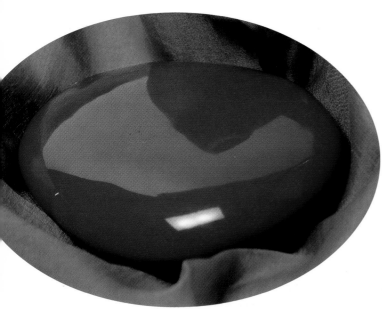

● *Red and green form a powerful combination.*

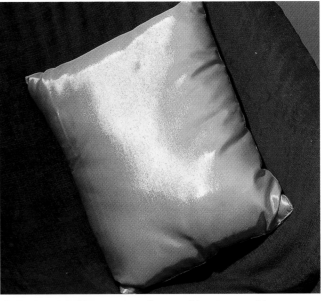

● *Red and gold are a popular combination, evoking richness and luxury.*

Red can be used with many colors, but if you are looking for inspiration, it is often a good idea to look to nature when considering color combinations. Red and green make a powerful, yet natural, marriage of colors. Reflected in nature by a ripe red apple on a tree, green holly leaves and red berries, and wild poppies in a green field, this strong color combination works very well in a traditional setting.

Reminiscent of Victorian interiors, a red-and-green room has a masculine air. Generally, the shades of red and green chosen for this style should be of an equal depth or tonal value; then the resulting scheme will be well balanced and even.

The Victorians also loved deep red and gold. They used this color combination as the perfect background for entertaining. All shades and tones of red look wonderful by candlelight, making it the ideal color for rooms used mainly in the evening. While red and gold are associated with riches and royalty, they can also be evocative of Eastern richness, as found in Oriental and Asian styling.

While less opulent, yet also very striking, red and white have been teamed together repeatedly throughout history, for instance, in porcelain, wallpaper, and fabric designs. Early 17th-century room schemes, for example, often featured red-and-white wallpaper and fabric. This color and design combination adds to the relaxed atmosphere. Toile de Jouy fabrics, hand-stitched, home-embroidered fabrics, checks, stripes, and flowing wallpaper designs are often found in red and white in this decorative style.

● *A red apple is a strong natural symbol.*

● *Red and gold are also evocative of Eastern richness.*

● *Red is one of the most popular and striking "accent" colors.*

Red and cream is also a combination with strong historical links. It is found in many period and regional styles. The popularity of cream was originally due to earlier manufacturing processes being unable to produce the bright white that we use today.

In interior design, decorators may use an additional color to "pep up" a scheme. This is known as an accent. Red is one of the strongest accent colors available to the home decorator as it can offer a striking contrast.

Throughout history, certain colors have waxed and waned in popularity according to the whims of contemporary fashions. Red is no exception.

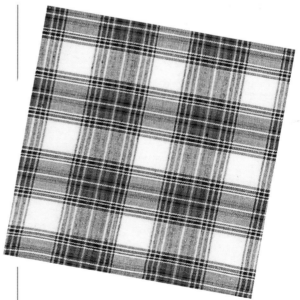

● *Red and white are often found in checked patterns, such as tartan.*

Blue

Blue, one of the primary colors, is known as the color of truth. It is representative of a higher mind and intelligence and is connected with both spirituality and emotions. As blue is considered the color of the higher consciousness, a dislike of this color may indicate that one is not being true to oneself and one's deep beliefs.

Blue is a restful color: it is cooling and calming. When someone is feeling overwrought, or if a person is prone to anger and anxiety, the wearing of this color will promote tranquillity and harmony of mind. Surrounding oneself with blues encourages contemplation, giving one the ability to calm the unquiet spirit and achieve an inner peace.

Symbolism

Blue is obviously associated with the sky, and hence with the sky father in many of the world's mythologies. It is because of this connection with heavenly divinity that some shades of blue are connected with the concepts of wisdom, rulership, and royalty. Blue is also the color of the seas and oceans and the feminine principle of boundless waters. Typically, images of the Virgin Mary, or the queen of heaven, are usually portrayed in blue. This symbolizes that she is a heavenly figure; she can also be identified with *Stella Maris*, the "star of the sea."

● *Blue is associated with the sky.*

In ancient China, several elemental powers characterized as dragons were considered to have associations with the color blue. The most obvious of these was the azure dragon, which was considered to be both the king of heaven and the symbol of the wood element: the emblem of the East, spring, growth, and creativity. On the other side of the world, the Celtic peoples of North-Western Europe regarded blue as the color of creativity; it was the sacred color of the bard or poet, the person who orally recorded the people's great deeds and heroic legends. The Mayans of Central America gave the color a less spiritual attribute: they used it to symbolize the deaths of fallen enemies.

Keywords for Blue

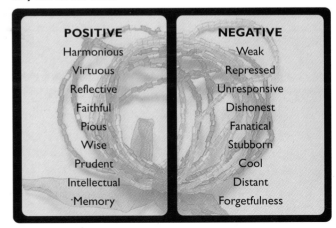

POSITIVE	NEGATIVE
Harmonious	Weak
Virtuous	Repressed
Reflective	Unresponsive
Faithful	Dishonest
Pious	Fanatical
Wise	Stubborn
Prudent	Cool
Intellectual	Distant
Memory	Forgetfulness

● *Blue is cool and calming, like the ocean.*

Astrology

In the system of astrological planets, blue—especially deep royal blue—is the primary color of Jupiter, the bringer of luck. The signs of Sagittarius and Pisces, both traditionally governed by Jupiter, are also associated with blue, and hence this color is considered to be particularly fortunate for those born under those signs. In the case of Sagittarius, the Archer, the shade is darker and more imperial, while the gentle, dreamy sign of Pisces, the Fish, inclines more toward aquamarine and watery tones.

Feng Shui

In the ancient Oriental art of Feng Shui, a distinction is made between light and dark blues. Light blue is considered to be interchangeable with green as a symbol of the East and its distinctive emblem of the dragon. Light blue is connected with the start of life, dawn, the season of spring, young children, newly grown buds, and fruitfulness. When blue is of a darker shade, however, it becomes interchangeable with black as a symbol of the North, of creeping cold and treacherous ice. In this more sinister mood, blue can be seen as the symbol of the end, rather

● *Dark blue has an association with cold and ice.*

than the beginning, of life. However, since the belief in reincarnation is found in many Oriental faiths, it is not so surprising that blue can be the symbol of both birth and death.

The Psychology of Blue

Blue is a cool color that has the psychological property of apparently making objects recede. Similarly, those who are possessed of a blue aura tend to dislike confrontation and will try to keep their problems at arm's length for as long as possible. Upsets and arguments are very distressing for a person with this aura, so it is not surprising that they are often too diplomatic for their own good.

If blue is dominant as a clothing color, or, indeed, as an aura color, then it is important that negative emotions are released slowly for fear of losing your temper and thus losing control.

● *Light blue is associated with the start of life.*

Blue and the Body

It is interesting to note that blue is associated with the throat chakra because it is used to treat many of the problems that occur in this area of the body. A psychological or spiritual problem is often reflected in the associated body part. If a person refuses to voice or deal with their problems or anger, the frustrated negative emotion will eventually spill out in an uncontrollable torrent, which can be traumatic for the person who loses their temper, as well as for the recipient. Other areas of the body that are affected and sometimes helped by being surrounded by, or bathed in, blue light are the upper arms, the base of the skull, and the thyroid and parathyroid glands.

Because of its associations with the astrological nature of Jupiter, blue is connected with expansion and thus, in physical terms, with weight gain. As a result, when using this color in light therapy, as, indeed, in everything else, moderation is important.

The Shades and Tints of Blue
Sky Blue

This tint of blue is among the calmest of the group. Sky blue denotes constancy, fidelity, and love. This color should be worn in times of trouble because it provides emotional help, enabling the wearer to overcome obstacles and win through to a peaceful and happy life. Sky blue promotes sensitivity and imagination. It can also boost a tendency to fantasize, sometimes allowing illusory achievements to replace real ones.

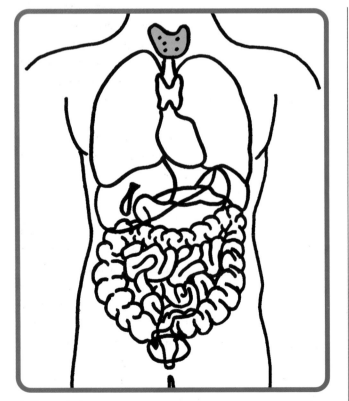

● *Thyroid gland.*

Azure Blue

This deeper shade of brilliant blue has connotations of contentment. However, this is not a passive state. People who are strongly influenced by azure blue are determined to achieve a great purpose, yet they know instinctively that the journey is better than the arrival at their destination. They enjoy their activities and will strive endlessly for goals—yet if they achieve all of them, they have to come up with more in order to maintain their contentment.

Pale Blue

Although this subtle tone hints at gentleness, in reality pale blue influences the ambitions and reflects an ability to reach for the sky. A person influenced by pale blue is inspired and has the ability to inspire others. In some ways, this type of person is a crusader, ready to strive for a great cause. He or she will also be magnanimous to foes and generous to friends. Wearing pale blue indicates an absolute determination to succeed.

Dark Blue

Lack of true communication is often a problem with those who habitually wear dark blue. Although this shade represents a calm, controlled nature, it also tends to indicate that a person is repressing their true feelings. People who are influenced by dark blue are prone to needless anxiety. This negative set of emotions can only be removed by discussing worries with those who are trusted. Herein lies the problem, because dark blue also suppresses the ability to give trust easily.

Blue in the Aura

As in Oriental tradition, the interpretation of blue in the aura is divided between the darker and lighter hues. Dark blue is usually an indicator of sound judgement, while the lighter tones suggest powerful intuition.

A person with dark blue as the dominant color of the aura will be reliable, honest, wise, and enterprising. Like dark green, this shade suggests someone who is go-getting and knows exactly where he or she is going, possibly a entrepreneur. This type of person is very ambitious, but this trait is tempered by a strong sense of compassion. Although they know exactly what they want, they are also sensitive to the needs and feelings of others and can be capable and wise advisors.

The negative side to dark blue is that one can lose touch with one's own feelings, focusing too heavily on the cerebral. The desire to make plans, to foresee every possible eventuality, can be overbearing and make a person seem too cold and distant for comfort. In this case, the wearing of dark blue indicates someone who is overstressed and preoccupied with problems.

If light blue is the dominant color in an aura, it indicates a nature that is artistic and refined. This tint is often found in the auras of painters, draftsmen, writers, actors, and other people involved in creative work. It implies an active imagination—in some cases, far too active. Light blue can also enhance the intuition, giving a powerful psychic awareness that may be felt on an unconscious level. This enables a person to be in tune with the feelings of those around them, possibly without actually being aware that interaction is taking place on a subtle, non-verbal level.

In times of stress, the habitual wearing of light blue is indicative of someone who has to make a lot of mental adjustments in a very limited period of time. It suggests insecurity and self-doubt. It may also show that a person is too accommodating to the desires of others because he or she is unsure of their own desires. Wearing light blue, or having this tint appearing in the aura, sometimes occurs when a relationship break-up is in the offing.

Color Combinations
Dominant Dark Blue and Yellow

If these colors are found in combination, then a period of mental clarity and optimism is about to occur. Someone who wears this striking combination is about to seize an opportunity that will lead on to great things. The interpretation is the same if these colors are spotted in the aura. Dark blue and yellow symbolize a sorting-out of priorities, a clearing of the decks, and a readiness to forge ahead. The combination also denotes a period of emotional clarity, of ditching the negative and embracing the positive in life.

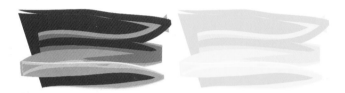

Dominant Light Blue and Orange

If this color combination appears in the aura, or if a person has taken to wearing this combination, they may well be in an overexcited state. There is a certain intensity about the personality of someone with this combination, and the need to communicate their deepest feelings has an air of desperation about it. There may be present a nervousness or nervous energy that leads to a remarkable bout of creativity. However, this period is rarely an easy one because the intensity of emotion may lead one to feel as if control is being lost. The conscious mind has to step back for a while to allow the true nature to emerge.

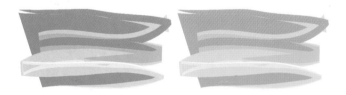

Dominant Dark Blue and Dark Green

The combination of darker shades of blue and green indicates a time of stress. This could be the result of overwork and strict deadlines, or, in some cases, of a difficulty in reconciling one's emotions to a difficult personal situation. There is the feeling that decisions made at this moment are absolutely crucial and that one cannot afford to make an error. If this combination occurs either in dress sense or in the aura, then it is time to step away from the rat-race for a while and relax.

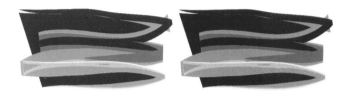

Dominant Dark Blue and Red

An air of expectancy surrounds a person who develops a red tone in an otherwise dark-blue aura. Such bold contrasts suggest that something big is forthcoming, and there is a sense of optimism about the personality. There may be excitement over an upcoming change of lifestyle: a promotion or perhaps the dawning of a passionate love affair. The fact that blue and red represent both cold and hot shows that the personality has developed a sense of balance.

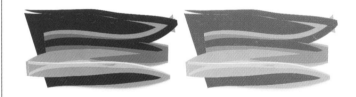

Dominant Light Blue and Pink

Light blue combined with pink often shows infatuation. Both of these colors are associated with childhood, and together they show an innocent, perhaps naïve, outpouring of emotion. This combination may also indicate a flirtatious personality, someone who is not in love with any particular person, but rather is in love with love itself. Unfortunately, there is likely to be an element of self-deception in such a personality because he or she might imagine affection from another when none exists.

Figures of Speech

Blue figures in many commonly used expressions, the most notable of which is "feeling blue." This phrase means to feel depressed, or, to be more precise, to be emotionally unfulfilled. Further to this, an entire musical genre was born in the Deep South, so to "sing the blues" often means to bemoan lost love or to protest against injustice. On the other hand, the "blue bird of happiness" expresses joy and has done so since the play of that name was first staged in London, England, in 1910.

Since blue is a color that expresses loyalty and high-mindedness, one can also be "true blue," meaning one who never betrays a trust; an

● *The blue bird often denotes joy.*

Oxford or Cambridge (University) Blue, an athlete; or even a "bluestocking," a misogynistic, 18th-century description of a female academic who was considered to have neglected her femininity in order to study—femininity and academic intelligence were believed to be utterly incompatible. There is also the expression a "blue-eyed girl or boy," which means to be highly thought of.

The Use of Blue in Decor

Blue is cool, peaceful, and refreshing, making it a color that is easy to live with. It is classed as a receding color, one that gives the illusion of space. It is therefore airy and expansive, indicative, perhaps, of the fact that in nature, blue is the colour of the bright, uplifting sky and the deepest ocean. Blue is also known to reduce the heart rate and is, by its very nature, ideal for creating relaxing interior schemes.

● *The term "bluestocking" was once used in a derogatory sense to describe a female academic.*

Blue is considered a formal color, possibly because it adds a cool quality to a room. The resulting space will appear calm, but not necessarily welcoming, unlike colors from the warm side of the color wheel.

You need only turn your attention to nature to appreciate the infinite possibilities for successful color combinations with blue. Imagine a Mediterranean scene, with its vivid blue sky as a background to pots of powerfully pink and red geraniums, or aromatic yellow lemon groves. Alternatively, consider the muted color combinations found in a coastal location: soft golden sand meeting shiny gray pebbles at the edge of reflective blue rock pools.

● *Blue and green are a popular combination in decorating.*

Blue and green are a pleasing, harmonious combination, echoed in nature by fresh blue flowers surrounded by varying colored leaves and stems. These colors offer a very balancing atmosphere to a room. And when used with paler tones of color, they create an extremely tranquil, yet focused, environment, ideal for a bedroom or study.

Pure reds contrast well with deeper blues in a strong scheme, and tints of red, in the form of pink, are a wonderful partner for paler blues in more subtle surroundings.

Strong red makes a powerful contrast when used with blue. It can be employed to great effect as an accent in a mainly blue color scheme.

● *Tints of red, such as pink, are excellent partners for blue.*

White is a traditional partner for blue, a combination seen repeatedly throughout history in blue-and-white porcelain and fabrics. It is possible that this fashion dates as far back as the 17th century, when the Chinese started exporting great quantities of porcelain to Europe.

● *A stem of fresh blue flowers represents a pleasing natural combination.*

Yellow and blue have become very widely used together. These contrasting colors from opposite sides of the color wheel offer a vibrant, yet balanced, mix. When seen in their purest, strongest form, they add strength to a room, reminiscent of the summer sun in a Mediterranean blue sky. Pastel lemon and soft sky blue add warmth and softness. Yellow and blue work best when the colors are tonally equal, but you must therefore be careful when planning your decor to ensure that the finished room has adequate tonal interest.

Various shades of blue are found in a wide range of historical or regional style interiors. Contemporary designers also enjoy its expansive quality. It is used to great effect when pinpointing areas within a design that would benefit from its receding effect. In this setting, blue is likely to be used in blocks, rather than *en masse*, as this would detract from the true power of the color. In a contemporary setting, less is undoubtedly more.

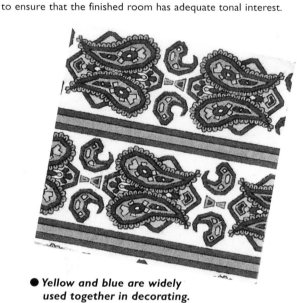

● *Yellow and blue are widely used together in decorating.*

● *Equal tones of color lead to a flat, uninteresting final effect.*

● *A tonal contrast in blue and yellow presents a fresh scheme.*

A room decorated completely in colors of an equal tonal value would be flat, uninteresting, and have little definition. You should therefore ensure that there is relief in the form of accent color and tonal contrasts. This will ensure life and vitality, and should result in a complementary decorative scheme.

The Victorians also had a place for blue within their palette. Deep royal blue was a favorite for wall coverings, fabrics, and ceramic tiles during that period. The Georgians before them also featured a select range of blue tones for their wall coverings and fabric ranges.

● *Eau de nil is a refreshing background color.*

Aquamarine

Aquamarine is a tertiary or intermediate color: it is produced by mixing together primary blue with secondary green. This is a relaxing and focused color as it harnesses many of the strengths associated with its parental colors, blue and green. It has an expansive air and is calming and serene.

Aquamarine has long been a favorite of interior designers and decorators. It has many guises, with various shades being suitable for use in both traditional and regional settings. The Georgians, for instance, favored such shades as eau de nil, the perfect background against which to display paintings and cherished items of furniture.

Brighter tones of aquamarine are associated with Mediterranean styling, emulating the color of the warm, Mediterranean sea and bringing a depth and richness to a scheme. Due to the bleaching effect of the sun, this color is also found in a more subtle form. Doorways and painted items take on a wondrously aged patina, bringing a new dimension to this color. Designers in America and Britain often attempt to recreate this look.

Aquamarine can be combined to great effect with such colors as violet, blue, cream, or white. When used in conjunction with natural products, such as timber, slate, and metallic finishes, aquamarine can offer the best of contemporary design.

Yellow

One of the primary colors, yellow is associated with the workings of the mind. Its bright, optimistic hue stimulates the intellect and curiosity. It is easy to see why yellow is considered to be the color of the scientist, the researcher, and of those who must concentrate. It is also symbolically associated with speed, especially speed of thought and quick decision-making.

If one is hesitant or unsure of one's next action, wearing or surrounding oneself with vibrant yellows will help to focus attention on the problem at hand and help to banish indecision. A lack of communication may also be addressed by the use of yellow. If a person is feeling lonely or unable to make meaningful contact with others, use of this bright hue will ease the flow of words and promote wit and style.

Symbolism

Yellow is one of those colors whose symbolism is contradictory. In its more positive aspect, it shares much of the symbolism of gold as

● *Yellow represents the sun.*

the color of the sun. However, in its darker shades, yellow derives much of its symbolic meaning from the fact that it is the color of urine.

● *Yellow is connected to newness.*

Its positive connotations are that it is considered the color of the intellectual, symbolizing the primacy of the mind over baser instincts. It has connections with newness, optimism, goodness, and fidelity. In its darker, more negative aspect, yellow denotes treachery, faithlessness, cowardice, and greed. This ambivalence is reflected in the character of the Roman god Mercury, the herald of the Olympian gods—from whose name the word "mercurial" comes. Although this deity was the trusted messenger of his father, Jupiter, he was also a deceptive and cunning influence on the lives of other gods and of men. On the one hand, Mercury is the god of trade and merchants; on the other, he is the deity of thieves and conmen.

In revolutionary France, yellow paint was daubed on the doors of people presumed to be traitors to the new regime. Yellow was also the color of the flag—the Yellow Jack—flown by a plague ship as a mark of quarantine.

Yellow has been used to symbolize heresy against the doctrines of the Catholic Church: "heretics" condemned to burn at the stake were often clothed in yellow as they met their grisly fate. Similarly,

members of the Jewish race were forced to wear yellow in medieval times. This practice was resurrected in Nazi Germany, where Jews were forced to wear a yellow star (a precursor to the horrors of the concentration camps).

Keywords for Yellow

POSITIVE	NEGATIVE
Alert	Evasive
Incisive	Preoccupied
Swift	Hasty
Focused	Obsessive
Honest	Cynical
Adaptable	Fickle
Witty	Sarcastic

Astrology

Swift thinking, curiosity, and a desire to communicate tie yellow into the astrological symbolism of the planet Mercury and its two signs of Gemini and Virgo. Mercury is also connected to travel, trade, and almost immediate perception.

Gemini is traditionally held to have the most in common with the color yellow. However, it can also be used by Virgos to good effect, lifting their often obsessive attention to detail. Yellow is said to help wearers to focus their mind on relevant facts rather than being swamped by irrelevancies. People who are born with Mercury, Gemini, or Virgo prominent in their horoscopes will find that yellow is a fortunate color for them.

Feng Shui

Yellow quite literally holds the central point in Feng Shui. In Chinese symbolism, yellow relates to the element of earth. It represents the central point of anything and is particularly relevant to health. Therefore a yellow carpet, ornament, or feature at the center of your home will promote wellbeing and help to restore order to your life.

In keeping with the central role of this color, yellow was also used to symbolize the emperor as the supreme authority of the state. In ancient China, the emperor alone was allowed to wear yellow; anyone else who had the temerity to do so could look forward to a spectacularly nasty demise. It is interesting to note that on the color wheel yellow and purple oppose each other—in the East, the color of imperial power was yellow, while in the West, purple performed the same function, symbolizing authority.

● *According to Feng Shui, a yellow ornament at the center of your house will promote wellbeing.*

Chapter 3 **Primary Colors**   **YELLOW**

The Psychology of Yellow

There is no doubt that yellow promotes joy. Just as a sunflower turns its face to the direction of the brightest light, so yellow itself will turn the mind toward optimism and happy memories. Yellow helps to promote clear, rational thinking. It also represents an accurate assessment of the realities of one's life. In cases of depression, being surrounded by this happy color will encourage more positivity and help people to gain an awareness of how to cope with their situation.

● *A sunflower is a perfect representation of the joy and brightness associated with yellow.*

Yellow and the Body

In terms of bodily parts, yellow is related to the stomach, in both Eastern and Western beliefs. We have already seen that yellow relates to the center of anything in Chinese belief, and in this case we can now consider the stomach to be the center of the body. The Chinese also hold that the stomach is the regulator of bodily functions and place great emphasis on cleansing and purifying the system with a healthy, balanced diet. Yellow foodstuffs, such as bananas, lemons, grapefruit, and corn, are not only great cleansing agents, but are also claimed to release inner tensions and provide a release from despondency.

In the mystical traditions of India, yellow is the color of the stomach chakra and again relates to balance. Organs that respond to the yellow vibration include the pancreas, spleen, digestive system, the skin, and the whole nervous system.

● *Yellow foods cleanse and revitalize one's system.*

The main use of yellow in color therapy is for the removal of toxins and the stimulation of the flow of gastric juices. Menstrual and other hormonal problems may also be eased by yellow light, yellow clothing, or simply by being surrounded by the color. Many color therapists use yellow to relieve diabetes, rheumatism, and eating disorders.

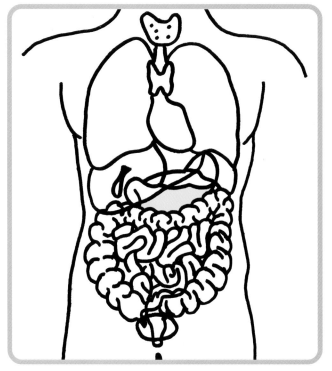
● *Stomach.*

The Shades and Tints of Yellow

Apart from the more generalized interpretations of this primary color, the shades and tints of yellow also have specific meanings of their own.

Dark Yellow

People who prefer the darker tones of yellow are often prone to feelings of low self-esteem. This may express itself as recurring bouts of despondency. Excessive grumbling is symptomatic of this type.

Lemon Yellow

Those who love lemon yellow are often loners. Self-reliant, they desire an orderly life and are very sensitive to criticism. However, they will prosper through being very astute.

Citrine Yellow

Lovers of citrine yellow are very changeable, not to say fickle; serial relationships are not uncommon with this type. Superficially clever, they are jacks of all trades and masters of (practically) none.

Primrose Yellow

Intense curiosity is the hallmark of those who love primrose yellow. Their interests are constantly homing in on often minor details that have captured their interest. This type often spends long periods in solitary pursuits and is very sensitive to discord and criticism.

Cream

Although cream could be considered a darker shade of white, its interpretation places it among the yellow group. Those who love the subtle shades of cream love new ideas and are open to novel influences. However, they need a lot of reassurance to be happy.

Yellow in the Aura

The appearance of yellow in the aura is differentiated between amber and a more lemony tint. Amber denotes people who are actively seeking a change in their lives. With this tone, the clarity of yellow is enhanced by the vibrancy of orange. It is the color of clear purpose and of strength of character. Amber expresses intelligence, perception, and originality, combined with a playful and joyful nature. If the dominant color of the aura is amber, or, indeed, a person displays a marked preference for this color, then courage in convictions is likely to be one of their main character traits.

Chapter 3 Primary Colors YELLOW

People with this color are very rational and can see that every cloud has a silver lining. Not only that, they are very adept at finding it with very little trouble. They possess a powerful sense of direction and tend to know exactly where they are going in life. In keeping with the mercurial qualities of yellow, people who favor lemon are very adaptable, and are often to be found engaged in several different activities at once.

The negative side of lemon is difficult to find, yet it can manifest itself as a manipulative quality and a readiness to make outrageous claims or tell plausible lies in order to achieve a necessary goal.

● *Wearing amber can represent a need to make the right impression.*

If a person goes through a period of wearing amber, it may be associated with getting a new and more fulfilling job, passing exams, or generally being concerned with making the right impression on those who matter. More negatively, amber can suggest arrogance.

When lemon is the dominant auric color, it is a healthy indication, signifying a vibrant attitude to life, physical wellbeing, and a happy personality: a person literally glowing with positive energies. This is not someone who will be brought down by needless self-doubt or the negative opinions of others.

Color Combinations

Dominant Amber and Light Green

This color combination, in dress sense or in the aura, indicates an eccentric personality who nevertheless possesses creative flair and the drive to succeed. This combination is found around people who enjoy what they do, are motivated, and love basking in the adulation of others. Yet this type does not take themselves too seriously and is willing to laugh at their own peculiarities, as well as being able to appreciate the follies of the world in general.

Dominant Amber and Red

A person with the combination of amber and red around them is a force to be reckoned with. Nothing is going to stand in this person's way for long. He or she can out-think, outpace, and outmaneuver any opposition with ease. This personality type is headed for the top, and woe betide any who should have the temerity to oppose this purpose. This aura is perceived around those who have achieved great things, the movers and shakers of this world who are capable of making far-reaching decisions without undue stress.

Dominant Lemon and Sky Blue

The combination of lemon and sky blue is indicative of a very responsive nature. It shows an open mind and a wonderful clarity of vision and understanding. This is not a person noted for cool calculation, but, on the contrary, someone lively, vivid, spontaneous, and enthusiastic. As usual with yellow types, this person has an active imagination, is prone to experiencing meaningful dreams, and is generally happy.

Dominant Lemon and Orange

There is a great urge for recognition in people who favor the combination of lemon and orange. They long to be noticed, looked up to, and appreciated for their wit, talent, and originality. However, they can be very critical of others, often envious of those who have achieved greater success than they, and very dogmatic in their opinions. Happiest in lively company, the lemon/orange-type person is often fearful of being alone for prolonged periods.

Chapter 3 Primary Colors YELLOW

Figures of Speech

Commonly, yellow is used as indicative of cowardice, for instance, the expression "yellow-bellied" is used to describe a coward.

The Use of Yellow in Decor

A primary color, yellow is vital, warm, and cheerful. In its purest form, it is reminiscent of the sun, bringing light and life into the darkest and dullest of spaces.

● *Yellow is often used in a range of natural colors.*

Yellow has become one of the most widely used colors in modern decorating. This does not, however, mean that it is a relatively new color for the interior designer. Bright yellow was first introduced during the early 19th century; teamed with black, it became widely used in a neoclassical setting. Prior to the introduction of this bright chrome yellow, natural pigments from ocher and raw sienna were widely used. These produced a mellow, glowing range of colors.

Yellow is easy to live with and can be an excellent decorative aid as it is strong enough to produce a substantial color scheme, one that is not overpowering or oppressive. Many rooms with little natural light can easily look claustrophobic and fussy, but a room decorated using shades of yellow can be made to look more spacious and stylish.

If you wish to use yellow as the base for monochromatic schemes, its success will lie in the use of adequate tonal variation. Varying tones and shades of yellow and a splash of noncolor, such as black or white, will look good.

Yellow and blue is a very balanced color combination for the home. It can offer a number of styling solutions, all giving a different atmosphere to a room. Sunshine yellow with rich blue is vibrant, modern, and uplifting, while a room decorated in buttermilk yellow and soft china blue can be very calming and will often capture a traditional air.

Yellow works best with blues of the same tonal value, or depth, as itself. This creates a very balanced, contrasting color scheme as the colors lie directly opposite each other on the color wheel.

Yellow and green offer a harmonious color partnership as they are found adjacent on the wheel. Picture buttercups in a green field to capture the ease with which these two colors combine effortlessly. Green can act as the perfect accent in a room decorated mainly in tones of yellow through to gold. Lime would be perfect in a contemporary, vivid-yellow setting, or sage in a more traditional room. If yellow and green are used in almost equal quantities within a color scheme, a third color may be required to add depth and contrast to the room. In this case, choose a color that lies opposite the yellow or green on the color wheel. Peach or terracotta, for example, would provide the perfect contrasting accent.

Pink can be a very powerful and exciting partner for yellow, creating a striking color scheme. Once again, I tend to mix colors of an equal tonal strength. In a contemporary setting, bright yellow and cerise work wonderfully. If the two colors are used in equal proportions, then just a splash of lime will tip the balance to create the perfect scheme. Yellow and rose or coral pink can create a fresh and sunny traditional environment. In fact, many archive floral chintz fabrics are found in these colors. In such rooms, grass green or light avocado offer the perfect accent color when needed.

The shade or tone of yellow that you choose should reflect the style or atmosphere that you are aiming to capture. There are many historical and regional styles incorporating yellow from which you can take inspiration. In the latter part of the Georgian period, colors became brighter and "Chinese yellow" became popular. Mustard was a favorite shade for the Victorians,

with the addition of gold embellishments, or contrasts of deep blue, dark green, or burgundy.

A traditional air is captured by "country-house-style" interiors. Here a number of shades of yellow can be found, inspired by country gardens. In this setting, many floral fabrics, which capture the yellows found in nature, are used as an anchor. The colors of the spring flowerbed offer a good color selection. These colors can look very effective when placed against a soft, sunny-yellow background.

● *Yellow and blue work well together.*

● *Terracotta and yellow produce a pleasing, rustic effect.*

The Mediterranean regions have a number of yellow shades and tones included in their distinctive color selections. In Provence, for example, the light and colors of Southern France provide opportunities to use sunshine yellow with Provençale red and rustic terracotta. The warmth of this shade of yellow is also used to great effect with vivid blue and olive green.

The Spanish palette includes many of the colors featured across the region as a whole. Here we find bright, vivid blues contrasting with sunshine yellow, olive green, and geranium pink. Meanwhile, the Greek color spectrum uses rustic ocher and sandy tones to capture the essence of this style.

To capture the warmth of Moroccan interiors, use earthy tones once again. Yellow ocher and such spice colors as turmeric yellow and rich saffron gold work beautifully with jewel colors and metallic finishes. The resulting schemes will replicate the rich heritage of this magical region perfectly.

Yellow can be an extremely effective tool for the modern decorator. It not only adds light and life to the space in which it is used, but it also lifts the spirits of those living within the color scheme. This makes yellow ideal for any room in the home. Imagine starting each day in a sun-filled bedroom; having a hallway that appears spacious and full of the vitality associated with an area drenched with sunlight; or a bathroom that is warm and lifts your spirits on the darkest of days. All this is easily achieved with the color yellow.

Chapter 4 Secondary Colors

Secondary colors are mixtures of at least two of the primaries. The secondary colors include green, a mixture of blue and yellow; orange, a combination of yellow and red; and the purple/violet range, combining the warmth of red with the cold of blue. The symbolism of these colors is often complex and contradictory, in keeping with their varied parentage.

Green

Green comprises a group of colors that are compounds of blue and yellow. It is primarily the color of lush vegetation, of new life, and springtime. The color also hints at the life-giving qualities of the sun (yellow), combined with the skies (blue), to bring new life to the world.

As green is the color of nature at its most abundant, it is therefore the color of reproduction, and thus of lovers. Bright green represents the hopefulness of young love, while darker tones represent envy and the negative emotions of love gone sour.

Symbolism

Although green is associated with growth and vegetation, its symbolism has certain ambivalent aspects. On the one hand, it has connotations of youthfulness and springtime, yet it is also the color of mold and decay. Because of this, green is associated with both the vernal hues of life and the livid horror of death. This is why, in some superstitions, green is considered to be a lucky color and in others it is considered unlucky. In Western Europe, green was believed to be the favorite color of fairies—not the tinsel-winged sprites of Victorian sentiment, but potent and willful powers who could condemn a person to bad luck if he or she should have the temerity to wear green. To this day, many people refuse to drive a green automobile, believing the vehicle to be more prone to accidents.

Keywords for Green

POSITIVE	NEGATIVE
Growth	Decay
Fruitful	Bitter
Tolerant	Suspicious
Talented	Envious
Fresh	Putrid
Lucky	Unlucky
Generous	Greedy
Loving	Jealous

Astrology

In Western astrology, green is associated with the earth signs of Taurus, Virgo, and Capricorn. Virgo and Capricorn tend to darker shades of the color, while the primary symbolism of green is reserved for Taurus and its ruling planet, Venus. In Roman mythology, Venus was the goddess of love, and likewise in astrology, the world of the emotions is strongly influenced by her color, green.

In astrological terms, both Venus and Taurus are associated with comfort and prosperity. Taurus, in particular, is said to govern property-owners, farmers, and bankers. In addition, people who are strongly influenced by Venus, or, indeed, born under Taurus, are said to be good with money and to possess "green thumbs," making them excellent gardeners.

● *Green is often considered a lucky color.*

Feng Shui

In Chinese tradition, green is interchangeable with light blue. (This concept is not unique to the Orient: the words for blue and green are the same in several Celtic languages.) The color green is emblematic of the East, the element wood, and the mighty green or azure dragon. The Eastern direction is also associated with the symbol *Chen*, or "thunder," signifying explosive growth. *Chen* can also be taken to mean "eldest son," and thus green becomes the symbolic color of an heir to an estate or fortune. It also has associations with a violent downpour of rain, which fertilizes the earth.

Green is made up of the primary colors yellow and blue. Blue contributes insight and vision, while yellow brings clarity and optimism, so green should be worn to encourage generosity, both of spirit and possessions. The color may also be usefully employed as an aid to memory. Wearing, or being surrounded by, this color will stimulate the powers of recall. However, an over-emphasis on the color may indicate difficulty in dealing with upsetting memories that prevent settling down to a contented way of life. There may be a conflict between the ideals and the emotional needs.

Like its primary star sign of Taurus, those influenced by green have the obstinacy and determination slowly, but surely, to solve this problem to their own satisfaction.

● *The color green can signify lightning strikes.*

However, in keeping with the ambivalent nature of green, this color can also signify flash floods and lightning strikes. The animals associated with the color are the cicada, the eagle, the swallow, and, of course, the dragon.

The Psychology of Green

Green is regarded as the great harmonizer. It is associated with the emotions and the positive or negative manner in which these may be expressed. Consequently, people who are influenced by green can often see both sides of any question, but usually have a strong moral sense of right and wrong. They can be rather judgmental, even though their efforts will invariably be idealistic and selfless.

● *Green can encourage generosity.*

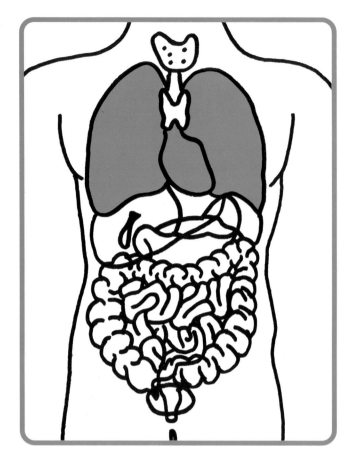

● *Heart and lungs.*

Green and the Body

Green is one of the most important healing colors because of its associations with new life and growth. Its primary organ is the heart, symbolically the home of love. It is also connected to the working of the thymus gland, the lower lungs, the chest, and the shoulders. Color therapists use green light as a tonic to combat fatigue.

Being bathed in this color is also said to combat nausea (being "green around the gills") and is helpful in restoring balance and soothing away headaches. It has been claimed that green can also alleviate cases of claustrophobia and is a help in coming to terms with traumatic memories.   Green vegetables, such as cabbages, cucumbers, peas, lentils and spinach, enhance physical stamina and are regarded as foods that cleanse the system.

The Shades and Tints of Green
Pale Green

Pale green is associated with youthfulness and a playful attitude. It also hints at an element of immaturity. In many cases, however, a childlike attitude is no bad thing since it provides the ability to give up on a bad job, to see things with new eyes, and to make a fresh start in life. Unfortunately, there is also a tendency to be indecisive, and people of this type may spend much of their time dithering about the best course of action to take.

Jade Green

In the Orient, jade is considered to be the most precious of all gems. Its color is therefore regarded as auspicious. Jade green is said to calm the spirit, to elevate wisdom, and to help a person to gain insight into the hidden workings of the universe. Even if one's aspirations are not quite that grandiose, the color still grants a philosophical outlook, combined with common sense. People who favor jade green are said to possess an enlightened nature.

Olive Green

Olive green hints at bitterness, of emotions gone sour, and resultant harm to the character. However, this color is not all bad news. It does indicate emotional pain, usually brought on by self-deception, but it also implies the strength of character to endure hard times and to come out the other side a better person. In consequence, a person who favors olive green

will be very caring about the feelings of others and will be beneficial in situations that need careful handling.

Emerald Green

This color is associated with the "Emerald Isle" of Ireland, so it is particularly favored by the Irish and those of Irish descent throughout the world. In terms of interpretation, this color is said to indicate material wellbeing combined with an easy-going nature.

Dark Green

Dark green primarily denotes a possessive character, and those who continually wear this shade of green are often self-obsessed and completely oblivious to the needs and desires of others. An over-emphasis on the darker side of green can indicate a life that is filled with remorse and regret. This type of person is likely to be harboring a long-felt resentment based on an early emotional trauma of some kind.

Green in the Aura

In terms of the aura, a difference is made in the interpretation of dark and light greens. Dark green is an indication of reliability, while light green suggests initiative. The general rule is that the darker the green, the more likely it is that the person is full of confidence.

A person with dark green dominant in his or her aura is a stable personality, perfectly able to cope in a crisis without becoming panicked in any way. Common sense and a pragmatic mind are obvious features of this type, as well as a love of nature. However, those with dark-green auras may not give themselves space to recuperate from physical or mental demands. They can also be very hard on themselves, rarely taking note of weariness or stress.

If light green is the dominant color of the aura, it is often indicative of someone who is wealthy, or one who works in the financial services or with cash on a daily basis. People with a light-green aura are practical and down to earth, but are less serious than their darker compatriots. However, they also may be far too eager to please other people without taking their own needs into account, and there may be a tendency to be tactless.

Color Combinations

Dominant Dark Green and Sky Blue

This is an imaginative combination, suggesting free-thinking and creativity. A person who displays this combination in their aura will also possess the practicality and drive to turn their dreams into reality. This combination also suggests an ability to cope with tight deadlines with ease.

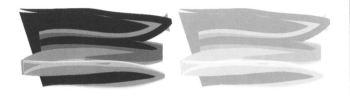

Dominant Dark Green and Red

This is an extremely passionate combination, often found in the auras of political leaders, captains of industry, and military commanders. This is an indicator of a risk-taker, yet this person is someone who carefully weighs up the odds before taking any drastic action. To the outside observer, he or she may seem reckless, yet every move is calculated. Even if the risky strategy does not work, there will usually be a get-out clause that allows this person to escape with little damage to either their person or their reputation.

Dominant Light Green and Blue

Artistic talent is shown when light green is combined with blue in the aura. This combination is often found around artists, creative writers, musicians, actors, and those who work with their hands. It is a combination that inspires and leads its fortunate possessor to greater and greater creative achievements. Unfortunately, this combination always doesn't guarantee recognition or any material rewards for one's efforts.

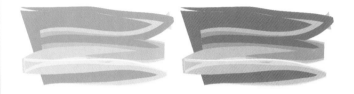

Dominant Light Green and Yellow

This is a combination that indicates a love of life and an exuberant spirit. For people with the combination of light green and yellow, life is a never-ending party. As long as there are interesting people to have fun with, this type of person will never be downhearted. This is a live-wire who can never sit still, one who is impatient, often with a short attention span and a need to be constantly on the move. They are also lovers of travel and adventure.

● *"Greenbacks" is a term for American dollars.*

Figures of Speech

There are probably more figures of speech connected with green than with any other color. To be "green around the gills" used to refer exclusively to seasickness, but can now refer to any form of nausea, including hangovers. Of course, due to the ambivalent nature of this color, one can be "green with envy" or experience the "green-eyed monster of jealousy."

On the other hand, one may be an excellent gardener and therefore possess "green thumbs." To "get a green light" is to receive the go-ahead on some project, while a "greenhorn" is a description of an inexperienced novice. In the theater, a waiting room for performers is called a "green room" because such rooms were originally painted in this restful color to relieve the eyes from the glare of the stage lights.

American dollars are often referred to as "the green stuff" or "greenbacks," due to the color of the currency first issued in 1862 during the American Civil War.

The Use of Green in Decor

Green is a secondary color, derived from the mixing of two total opposites, yellow and blue. It is balanced and very harmonious. It is this quality that has led to it being used for decorating "green rooms" in the theater as it produces a very steadying and contemplative room, ideal for calming nerves.

Green is associated with nature, it is easy on the eye, relaxing, and very versatile. Many tones and shades of green can be combined within one color scheme, and they will work as harmoniously within the home as they do in nature. This natural association is very obvious in the names chosen to describe the various shades and hues available to the home decorator: apple, grass, lime, sage, and avocado, to name just a few.

Green is the ideal color for decorating studies and home offices, where concentration is important. Due to the fact that its parent colors, yellow and blue, are of an equal strength, green is a very balanced color. This offers a calm and steadying quality to both a room and a room's inhabitants.

Greens with a very yellow base, such as lime, have an uplifting quality. Rather like the yellow-green shoots of new young leaves, this shade creates a very optimistic, stimulating atmosphere. The essence of this color is ideal for young, modern-style interiors, or for use as an accent within a scheme.

Green is sited on the cool side of the color wheel, which means that many lighter tones are ideal

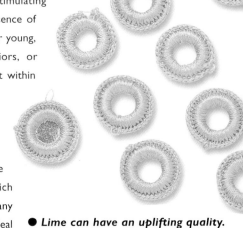

● *Lime can have an uplifting quality.*

for adding a spacious appearance to a room. While this color is not as receding as blue, it nevertheless offers a more expansive atmosphere than colors from the warm side of the color wheel.

Greens with a blue base, like aquamarine, take on some of the restful qualities of its blue parent color. Calming and expansive, these are ideal to use in a room dedicated to total relaxation.

● *The combination of green and red is often found in tartan.*

Room schemes that combine green tones or shades with creams and white capture the quality of the preferred color to best effect. Depending on the specific colors chosen, the resulting room will be calming, restful, or contemplative, never over-fussy or oppressive.

As in nature, green works extremely well with most other colors. Harmonious color combinations are found adjacent to green on the color wheel. Green with blue-green and yellow-green offer a very natural, relaxing scheme. The strongest color partner for green is red. Directly opposite on the color wheel, this is green's most striking contrasting color and can produce a very powerful scheme when used in its purest and strongest form. Red and

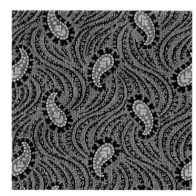

● *Green paisley is another traditional design.*

green were often found in a Victorian setting. Masculine and strong,

this is the ideal option for a decorator wishing to capture the essence of this period style. The combination is found in many traditional furnishing fabrics, such as tartans, checks, and paisley designs.

Tints of green and red in the form of pink and soft green offer a very delicate and complementary partnership and are ideal when used in small-floral-printed wallpaper and fabrics for a country-style room. For stronger effect, some modern designers use the powerful combination of vivid pink and lime green.

Terracotta and earthy shades of burgundy can combine with soft green to produce Provençale-style interiors. This warm, yet restful, combination is ideal for people wishing to capture the essence of rustic French style. Blue, green, and yellow are also found in many Provençale-style designs of fabric and rustic china.

● *Green with terracotta and other earth shades is very reminiscent of French rustic style.*

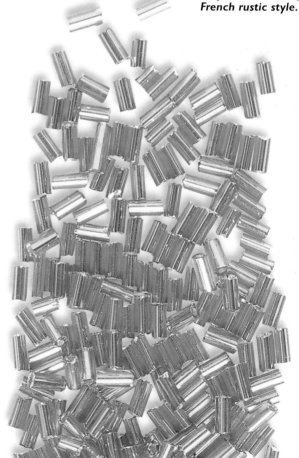

Green and orange, the color from which terracotta is derived, also work very well together. They offer an interesting contrast between the balanced nature of green and the sociable and stimulating character of orange.

● *Green and terracotta work well together.*

Contemporary style has seen the introduction of soft greens to the neutral palette in recent years. The addition of green to a mainly cream-and-white scheme has added a new dimension to this simple, yet elegant, type of color scheme.

Traditional country-house-style interiors use many tones, tints, and shades of green to great effect. Green reflects the surrounding countryside, an element that has so often inspired designs for this style of decor. This is why there are so many fabric and wall-covering designs incorporating shades and tones of green, combined with other colors that are found in a natural setting.

To achieve a Mediterranean style, use such shades as olive and lime green within colour schemes; when seeking to recreate the look of a particular region, plants that occur naturally within that geographical area, and their fruit, provide the perfect inspiration.

Or look to the architecture and decor of the region itself, for instance, bright aquamarine can be found in vibrant combinations in both Moroccan- and Turkish-style interiors. These schemes include a palette of jewel colors, often taking inspiration from the colors used in early Islamic art.

● *Retro style often features aquamarine, as well as more vibrant colors.*

Aquamarine

Aquamarine is an intermediate or tertiary color, found where blue and green meet on the color wheel. This color has been particularly popular in recent years, featuring heavily in modern-style interiors. It has, however, been used throughout history, and has connections with ancient Islamic artwork and interior decor from the Georgian period, as well as being popular in regional-style interiors. Here, soft, duck-egg blue, a color with a slightly green undertone, is used widely.

Nineteen-fifties', retro style also benefits from the use of aquamarine within its color palette. A full-bodied version was often used for kitchen furniture of the period. The color was also combined to good effect with sage and acid green in many fabric and printed designs.

Aquamarine and peach, soft cream and mint, lemon and lime, sage and terracotta—the combinations for home decorating and design in general, using different greens, are endless. Green is an extremely versatile color, ideal if you need to transform a room, that can offer infinite color-scheming possibilities.

Orange

Orange is a mixture of red and yellow, said to combine passion with flair. Orange is the color of assimilation, of testing, of judging, and of acceptance or rejection. It is considered to be a genial color, representing tender feelings, a warm heart, and friendship. Orange is also said to help to break down barriers, to remove obstacles, and to allow turbulent feelings to be resolved. Its yellow component ensures that this process is performed rationally, by muting the impetuous nature of red.

Being surrounded by this hue will broaden perspectives. It will give one the courage to make necessary changes and to accept the consequences of one's actions. People who are very strongly influenced by the vibration of orange will never be content to leave an unsatisfactory situation untackled. In this sense, orange is a revolutionary color, and those under its influence will be ready to move heaven and earth to make sometimes drastic improvements. In addition to this, they will have all the persistence they could possibly need to see the project through to a successful conclusion.

● *The color orange represents splendor in the traditions of ancient Egypt.*

Symbolism

In essence, orange is regarded as the color of the sunset (pink being symbolic of the dawn). It is also associated with grandeur and the tawny desert landscape. Visualize the pyramids of Egypt at dusk, with the warm, orange glow of the setting sun illuminating the scene, to get some idea of the magnificence symbolized by this color.

● *Orange is associated with the desert landscape.*

● *Orange can represent luxury.*

In the traditions of both ancient Egypt and Jewish mysticism, orange represents splendor. It is also symbolic of fire, and, in keeping with Egyptian symbolism, of the lioness-headed goddess Sekhmet, the courageous daughter of the sun god, Ra. Orange can be used to represent the concept of luxury, of living one's life to the full in comfortable surroundings. In both Chinese and Japanese traditions, orange is one of the primary symbols of love and happiness.

scholars to have been the fruit of the Tree of Knowledge of Good and Evil with which Eve tempted Adam in the Garden of Eden (a fruit more traditionally assumed to have been an apple).

● *The peach is symbolic of immortality.*

● *Oranges represent a zest for life and the power of the sun.*

Orange fruits have their own particular meanings. The peach is symbolic of immortality, or at least longevity; oranges represent both a zest for life and the power of the sun. The apricot (though some say that it is the humble dried fig) also has a set of associations, ranging from being the emblem of Egyptian queens to being believed by many ancient

Keywords for Orange

POSITIVE	NEGATIVE
Energetic	Indolent
Tender	Insensitive
Brave	Reckless
Genial	Overbearing
Generous	Extravagant
Proud	Vain
Liberal	Immoral
Persistent	Stubborn

● *People associated with both Leo and orange are often excellent with children.*

these people, and they usually develop marvelous relationships with children.

In more adult relationships, the Leo/orange connection has strong associations with romantic dalliance, and people dominated by the sign and/or the color are usually outrageous flirts. Any competitive urge will be channeled into sporting activities, and people of this type are often keen swimmers. Another talent that the Leo/orange type excels at is cookery.

Feng Shui

In common with Western symbolism, Feng Shui makes a connection between orange and the regal lion. However, the Orient also extends this noble symbolism to include the tiger and the horse. These images are considered to be lucky for those who have an affinity with orange. The compass direction associated with orange is the North-West, which comes under the rulership of the metal element. This area is known as *Chien*, the Creative, and is particularly

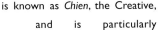

Astrology

In astrological terms, orange has much in common with metallic gold as a solar color. Orange also has a particular affinity with the zodiacal sign of Leo, the Lion. Like the sign, orange has the reputation of encouraging extrovert ideals, creativity, and self-promotion. The kindly nature of both Leo and orange cannot be overstressed because the motives of those influenced by both are generally very good. They often have the highest motives and are very compassionate, yet can simultaneously be insensitive, often preferring to act on other people's behalf without actually taking the views of those whom they wish to help into account. There is a distinctly "parental" aspect to

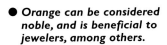

● *Orange can be considered noble, and is beneficial to jewelers, among others.*

 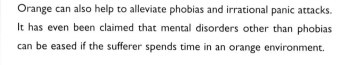

beneficial to lawyers, managers, jewelers, sales people, teachers, priests, psychoanalysts, counselors, and all those who take up a position of responsibility and leadership.

The Psychology of Orange

In color therapy, orange helps to remove psychological blockages. Deep, despondent feelings of grief and a sense of loss following bereavement can be alleviated by this warm, comforting hue. Orange can impart emotional strength, which enables one to withstand hardships. In the aftermath of a sudden loss, many people feel as though they are psychologically paralyzed, and view the world with fear. This inability to cope or move forward from the distressing event will be helped by bright sunshine and this splendid color.

Orange can also help to alleviate phobias and irrational panic attacks. It has even been claimed that mental disorders other than phobias can be eased if the sufferer spends time in an orange environment.

Orange and the Body

Orange relates to the lower intestines, and, by extension, to the "gut instincts." Bowel disorders and intestinal cramps may be alleviated by orange light to aid the assimilation of nutrients into the system. Orange is credited with helping things to flow, removing blockages, and making necessary changes, therefore being surrounded by orange is said to help to keep one's digestive system moving smoothly. As well as the intestinal associations of the color, orange light will aid the healing process of deep muscle aches, torn ligaments, and broken bones. It is also said to be therapeutic for breathing problems, such as asthma and bronchitis.

● *Orange can impart emotional strength.*

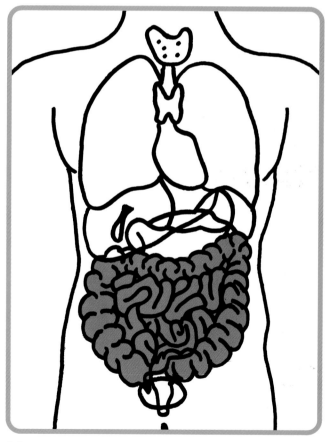

● *Intestines.*

The Shades and Tints of Orange

Peach

Lovers of peach usually possess impeccable manners, are rarely at a loss in any situation, and are great communicators. They have natural charm and grace and will do their level best to put other people at their ease. If there is a fault to be found, it is that lovers of peach may sometimes be too anxious to please, and often put other people's desires before their own, even when the situation calls for more self-assertion.

Amber

Those who lack confidence would be well advised to wear amber to enhance their self-esteem. This color is also useful when one suffers from anxiety or is apprehensive about a forthcoming event. It can signal a need to compose oneself in order to maintain an outward appearance of calm authority. There is an air of anticipation about this color.

As an auric color, amber may signal a hint of arrogance about the character. However, this will also be a person who is actively seeking improvements and positive developments in his or her life. Anyone with a strongly amber aura has great courage in their convictions and will not shy away from conflict. This color is also evident around people who are convinced that their way is the only right way.

Terracotta

Despite its great popularity in interior decoration, terracotta and, indeed, dark oranges in general do not have a very positive interpretation. They can speak either of overconfidence or the undermining of self-esteem. Both possibilities have the same outcome, that of failure, and ultimately the feeling that one is a loser. In addition, the dark oranges have associations with gambling.

Orange in the Aura

An orange aura is associated with originality, creativity, and self-motivation. An orange glow surrounding a person suggests that he or she is a friendly, extrovert sort of person, with a great deal of willpower, the ability to make the most of any opportunity, and, in many cases, to occupy the limelight. This last is particularly true if orange is the most dominant color in the aura. If orange should occur in patches throughout the aura, it is an indication of wit and liveliness, of someone who is a natural communicator and genuinely interested in what others have to say.

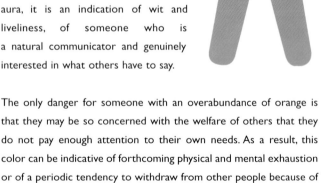

The only danger for someone with an overabundance of orange is that they may be so concerned with the welfare of others that they do not pay enough attention to their own needs. As a result, this color can be indicative of forthcoming physical and mental exhaustion or of a periodic tendency to withdraw from other people because of emotional overload.

Color Combinations

Dominant Orange With Red, Maroon, or Scarlet

This combination is indicative of someone who has all the potential to be a great success, but has not yet achieved the heights that he or she instinctively knows that they can attain. If this combination occurs for long periods of time, there may be a sense that natural destiny has been blocked in some way. On the other hand, a momentary frustration, such as missing a train or picking the wrong lottery ticket, may produce this combination of colors in a brief outburst of pique.

Dominant Orange With Lavender, Mauve, or Lilac

This combination, from opposite ends of the color wheel, often indicates that the normally exuberant orange personality is worn out. It shows a desperate need to take things easy and to recharge the batteries. A feeling of being irreplaceable is common when this combination is seen. However, in terms of work, duties, and general responsibilities, no one is truly irreplaceable. This person should take a backseat for a while and let someone else deal with their currently overwhelming responsibilities.

Figures of Speech

Orange has few associations with figures of speech, yet the color has occasionally found its way into common expressions. The most notable of these is found in British and Irish history in connection with "King Billy" or King William III. He was a Dutchman, of the princely house of Orange. Hence the Orange Order was founded in Ulster, Northern Ireland, in 1795 in commemoration of that king's victory at the Battle of the Boyne in 1690.

The Use of Orange in Decor

The color orange is vital and strong. It is a color seen in nature, not only in the form of the setting sun and glowing flames, but as its namesake, the zesty citrus fruit, ripened in the warm sun. Being a secondary color, orange has many of its parent colors' attributes – the cheerfulness of yellow, combined with the heat and attractiveness of red. No wonder, then, that orange is a warm color, ideal for introducing a sociable, temperate glow to a room.

Orange is a very powerful color. It can lift your spirits in the same way as yellow. It also inherits some of the power associated with red, thus resulting in a color that is thought by many to be able to stimulate the immune system and offer general healing powers.

Large areas of this color should be avoided within the home as orange can make a room appear too intense and overstimulating. If you decide to use orange on the walls of a room, consider a wash of color. This will deliver the color in a softer manner, while still retaining its warmth. Shades of colour derived from orange, such as terracotta or apricot, or individual blocks of color, may be another solution.

● *Rustic or country-style decor often benefits from terracotta tones.*

All shades, tones, and tints of orange can be used to great effect with many other colors from the color wheel. When combined with mellow greens, earthy terracotta creates a very natural, welcoming color scheme. Vibrant orange, however, can be used with bright blues, limes, or violet to create a very contemporary space within the home. Lively and uplifting, this type of scheme is ideal for rooms in which you socialize, or spend time as a young, busy family. This is not a color conducive to relaxation and calm tranquillity.

Rustic shades of orange, such as terracotta, can work very well in a traditional setting. As orange is an advancing color, it can be used to make large, austere rooms into more comfortable and welcoming environments. Traditional dining rooms

● *Shades of orange can be used to great decorative effect with many other colors.*

and rustic-style kitchens can greatly benefit from this color scheme. Not only will the space appear cozy, but the sociable nature of this color will ensure that the room's inhabitants feel comfortable and confident.

As orange is such a stimulating color, it is ideal for the decoration of children's playrooms; it is lively and invigorating, as well as being warm and comforting. While orange is not the most relaxing of colors on the color wheel, it is still widely used when producing color schemes for children's bedrooms. It may not help to soothe your child to sleep at night, but this wonderful color should encourage them to wake inspired and full of enthusiasm for the day ahead.

Orange and violet are a strong, modern combination that works best with ample contrast. The addition of white and black to a scheme is very effective.

Orange shades and tones have been used throughout history. The first colors were derived from natural pigment, resulting in earthy tones of terracotta. As manufacturing processes improved, paler apricots and peach were followed by the many "new" colors seen today. The 21st-century home-decorator has a wider selection of colors than has ever been available before.

● *Terracotta is derived from a natural pigment.*

Technically speaking, brown is not a secondary color: it is actually a "tertiary." In other words, it is the combination of three primaries rather than just two. However, in terms of symbolism, brown is considered to be a darkened pigment of orange and shares much of its significance, albeit in a darker, more sober and responsible manner.

Like its parent color, brown denotes warm feelings and friendship, yet its darker shade also hints at permanence and worthwhile values that stand the test of time.

Symbolism

Practicality is one of the foremost concepts associated with brown. This is a color with no frills or fancies. Those who express a preference for brown are often considered to be unimaginative, dull, and straight-laced. Yet when a job needs doing well and with care, these are the people who get on with it and, equally importantly, stick to it through thick and thin until it is completed. Of course, such demanding efforts often take their toll, even when, as is usual, the tasks symbolized by brown are successfully accomplished. Melancholy, a feeling of malaise, being put-upon, and generally persecuted are often associated with prolonged effort. In the French

language, *brun* often possesses a lackluster connotation of gloom, while, in Britain, the expression "browned off" means to be generally world-weary and unhappy.

On a more positive note, brown can invoke feelings of comfort and luxury. There is often a sense of richness associated with brown. It is, after all, the color of chocolate, coffee, and tea—welcome antidotes to a trying day. The sense of security provided by brown should not be underestimated. Building materials, such as bricks and natural woodwork, evoke a sense of permanence and safety. In terms of physical health, too, most people would rather be bronzed by the sun than pale and listless, despite all medical warnings to the contrary.

Keywords for Brown

POSITIVE	NEGATIVE
Studious	Nit-picking
Dedicated	Stubborn
Comforting	Despondent
Practical	Persecuted
Dutiful	Martyr to others

Astrology

Brown is associated with the colors of fall. Its rich hues indicate a period when the earth has given up its fruitfulness in the harvest and now prepares for its winter rest. This connection with the harvest points to the astrological sign of Virgo, a sign associated with duty and hard work. Equally, the symbolic capacity of those who love brown to accomplish great things indicates another earth sign, Capricorn, the Goat.

Feng Shui

In terms of Feng Shui, brown is an earth color mainly associated with the South-West and the trigram *Kun*. It represents the fertile soil and roots that grow in the rich darkness. The color is said to be beneficial to those who fulfill a maternal role or are carers, in the medical professions, gardeners, grocers, farmers, and civil engineers.

The Psychology of Brown

On a more general note, brown is said to be a particularly fortunate color for students to wear because it aids concentration and dedication to the task in hand.

Violet and Purple

A combination of red and blue, violet is considered to be one of the most spiritual colors. It implies harmony between the mind and emotions, between the divine and the physical. However, in the symbolism of color, there is little differentiation between violet and purple, so we have chosen to combine them into a single section in this book.

Symbolism

Purple's primary association is with royalty, and most especially emperors. For millennia, this color has been symbolic of worldly power, considered to be the preserve of the highest imperial authority, such as the emperors of ancient Rome. For lesser persons to presume to wear purple was considered such an insult to the emperor that the crime was often punishable by death.

As well as representing the highest form of earthly aristocracy, purple and its cousin, violet, symbolize an aristocracy of the spirit. The two colors are associated with great vision, spiritual illumination, and psychic abilities.

Keywords for Violet/purple

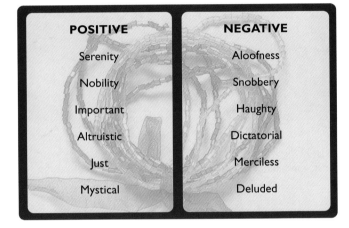

POSITIVE	NEGATIVE
Serenity	Aloofness
Nobility	Snobbery
Important	Haughty
Altruistic	Dictatorial
Just	Merciless
Mystical	Deluded

Astrology

The strongest astrological association of purple is with the visionary sign of Sagittarius, the Archer, while violet is more commonly connected to the mystical sign of Pisces, the Fish. Both of these zodiacal signs are influenced by the planet Jupiter, named after the king of the Roman gods, the archetypal emperor.

● *Purple is a symbol of the divine.*

Feng Shui

There is little in the way of Oriental symbolism for either purple or violet, but perhaps this is not so difficult to understand when one considers that Feng Shui is the art of living in harmony with the natural world. The symbolism of both purple and violet is essentially heavenly, and relates to more subtle realms of existence beyond our sphere.

The Psychology of Violet and Purple

The constituent elements of violet and purple are red and blue. These two are far apart in the spectrum and thus express very different traits, both psychologically and emotionally. It is this very difference that elevates violets and purples beyond the physical realms into the more spiritual realities.

● *Purple or violet can encourage calmness and peace.*

Being surrounded by violet or purple encourages a calm and peaceful state of mental reflection. People who prefer these colors tend to be thoughtful and rather introverted. They also show great depth of feeling, not just on a personal level, but also in a more universal sense, indicating a love of humanity in general, as well as caring for the environment and the state of the planet. Wearing violet or purple can be used as a defense mechanism against insensitive people, or against those who make excessive demands.

In a more negative sense, being constantly surrounded by violet or purple can prove to be a depressive influence because their energies are so strong that the mind cannot cope with an overload of these hues. If a person has suffered from depression because of exposure to too much purple, the cure lies in being exposed to golden and orange hues.

Violet and the Body

In terms of the human body, violet and purple strongly relate to the functioning of the brain. These colors also relate to the skull, most especially to the top of the cranium and the scalp. In recent times, the identification of violet with the crown chakra has led to it being linked with the pineal gland, the so-called "third eye," which regulates the hormonal balance of the body.

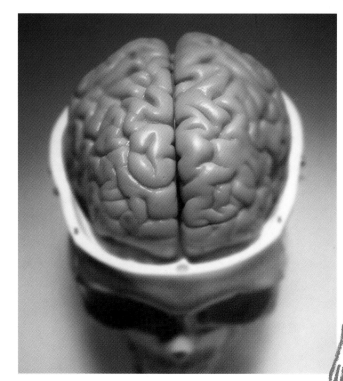

● *Violet and purple relate to the functions of the brain.*

Purple foods, such as eggplants, are said to be therapeutic for any kind of internal inflammation, as well as easing problems associated with the scalp and hair loss. The immune system and nervous tension may be treated with violet or purple light. However, neither purple nor violet lighting and clothing are recommended for children because both colors can short-circuit their natural development and encourage too much precocity.

● *Purple foods are said to be therapeutic.*

The shades and tints of violet and purple

Indigo

A preference for indigo is said to indicate a state of constantly waiting for something to happen, which, in many cases, turns out to be fruitless. Indigo might denote the belief that it is always darkest before the dawn, with the dawn never seeming to arrive.

Deep Purple

This is the color of emperors, of power and might. As might be imagined, there are overtones of arrogance and superiority about deep purple, as well as a fair degree of ruthlessness.

Amethyst

This tone promotes idealism, humanitarianism, and mystical trains of thought. People who prefer this shade are intuitive and often possess a sense of destiny.

Mauve

Mauve is a color that helps one to make the right choices for the best possible reasons. There is a paternal influence at work here, which may express itself in terms of aristocratic traditions and is concerned with the furtherance of a dynasty or a deeply held belief system.

Plum

Plum tones hint at an old-fashioned way of doing things. Plum may indicate someone who is a stick-in-the-mud, with prudish attitudes and outworn ideas. On a positive note, it indicates a sense of honor.

Lavender

There is a certain fragility about people who love lavender. This color hints at great perception, but also vulnerability. Lavender is said to enhance one's tastes, making those who prefer this color extremely esthetic in nature.

Lilac

Those who love lilac also love glamour. They possess a bright, outgoing personality, are rather vain, and are extremely fashion conscious. Romantic and flirtatious by nature, lilac lovers never lose an air of youthfulness.

Violet in the Aura

When found in the aura, violet and purple express the ethereal and the magical. An aura that is mostly violet indicates a person who finds deep spiritual meaning in their existence. It can also reveal humility and a martyrlike acceptance of life's troubles. These colors also represent a powerful imagination, a spontaneous personality, and a certain quirky way of looking at the world. Violet is often found in the auras of people with clairvoyant or a medium's abilities.

In combination with any other color in the aura, violet indicates a more spiritual dimension that transcends the mundane.

● *A florid writing style is often described as "purple prose."*

Figures of Speech

Violet is not really associated with figures of speech. However, the flower that shares its name has become an emblem of humility, despite its mythical origins: it is said to have sprung from the blood of the boastful hero Ajax during the Trojan War. Purple, on the other hand, is fairly common as a figure of speech. To "assume the purple" was a euphemism for inheriting the throne; to "attain the purple" refers to being made a cardinal of the Roman Catholic Church. Similarly, to be "born to the purple" is to be born to an important, or royal, family. In a literary context, "purple prose" is an over-florid style of writing, which could be said to send critics into a "purple passion."

The Use of Violet in Decor

Violet is sited where cool and warm colors meet on the color wheel; because its parent colors, blue and red, have an almost equal strength of color, it can be both warm and cool. If the shade being used is predominantly blue, it will appear cool, whereas if it has a redder base, it will appear warm. Green is similarly sited on the wheel, but blue dominates the mixture of yellow and blue that creates this color. Green is therefore a cool color.

The perceived warmth of your chosen shade of violet will depend on the colors with which you combine it. If you choose a lavender blue and combine it with pink, the lavender will appear cool. If you combine the same shade with blue, it will look considerably warmer as the red within the lavender will become more obvious.

Certain deeper shades and tones of violet can be very intense and should therefore be used cautiously and treated with respect. A room painted throughout with this type of color will need adequate relief to be successful. It is often more effective to tone down the color, use a pastel shade, such as lavender, or use it sparingly as a block within a room.

Tints of purple, that is, purple with white added, sit very comfortably with various shades of pink. Pink is a red tint, that is, red with white added. This means that it sits next to violet on the color wheel, making them a harmonious color partnership. Blue and violet offer an equally harmonious partnership:

pale shades of blue and soft lavender create a very calm, relaxing atmosphere.

Aquamarine and purple are a popular, modern combination. They sit together extremely comfortably, with paler shades offering a very relaxing, calm environment. This partnership works well because various shades and tints of blue are naturally harmonious partners for violet and purple. As with many two-color schemes, one of the colors should dominate, or an accent will often be required. In a contemporary setting, a metallic accent, such as the introduction of silver accessories, would work extremely well.

● *Purple works wonderfully with white.*

Pale shades, such as lavender, are fresh, soothing, and uplifting, the perfect colors to add a countrified vitality to a scheme. Lavender works beautifully with white, giving a room a crisp freshness. Alternatively, it can add a very contemporary twist to a room when teamed with yellow, green, or sharp lime. A number of archive fabrics are produced in purple or lavender. Many of these are a single color on a cream or off-white base. The traditional toile de Jouy designs are one such example. A clever designer could combine

a fabric like this with a contemporary accent color, such as lime, to produce an essentially traditional scheme that has a wonderful, contemporary edge.

Purple returns to fashion repeatedly as a color for home decorating. In my own lifetime, I have seen it used as part of three design cycles. During the 1960s, flower power brought mix-and-match floral and psychedelic designs into interiors, a very strong theme of which was shades of purple and pink.

● *Purple has been a popular ingredient of psychedelic designs.*

The mid-1970s saw the introduction of a stronger shade of purple used in a block on individual, often textured-finished, walls, which were normally surrounded by simple, white paintwork. This period saw many fabric designs incorporating larger-scale, repeating motifs and simple, textured fabrics featuring purple. The 1990s saw yet another revival of this color when it was introduced into many furnishing fabrics and wall coverings. This time the effect was much softer as we experienced harmonious combinations of aquamarine and purple, soft green, and lavender.

There is a strong connection between fashion and interiors. If you look back over the last thirty years, there is a strong link between the colors used on the runway and those that dress our homes. This has, in fact, always been the case. At each stage in history, contemporary designers have been inspired by prominent events and discoveries of their day.

Prior to the 19th century, deep violet was commonly used, making way in the early 19th century for pale colors, such as lavender, to become popular. Following the invention of aniline dyes during the 1840s, designers had a broader palette available to them, and deeper colors once again became fashionable. This is when purple reappeared, alongside deep blue, acid green, and mustard.

Contemporary manufacturing processes have introduced the widest range of colors ever available to designers. This is why so many design trends can co-exist as the interior designer is able to replicate so many regional and historical styles.

Chapter 5 Noncolors

Moving away from the bright hues of the color wheel, we enter a strange area of noncolor. Here we find the stark contrast of black and white, as well as the misty enigma of gray. Although white is technically the combination of all colors, and black the total absence of color, we tend to regard them as completely separate, of relevance only in regard to each other. Gray, on the other hand, is the combination of both of these extremes, and our attitude to this "shadow color" is most revealing.

Gray

Gray stands midway between white and black, between absolute yang and ultimate yin. It can be described as a "shadow color" because, like the absolutes that create it, gray does not appear in the color wheel. The result of mixing white and black, gray is an ambivalent color. When expressed as a mood, it is often bleak and grim, yet it does have a more optimistic outlook as a neutral. Gray is open to new influences and provides a bridge for the conscious and unconscious minds. This gateway can have both positive and negative connotations. On the one hand, gray can represent an access to the psychic levels of the mind; on the other, it may indicate despair.

● *Gray can be associated with the cold, harsh North Sea.*

sometimes revealing what lies ahead, but most often concealing the truth.

Paradoxically, although gray is the "messenger" color, it is also associated with silence, and sometimes with grief. The Norse peoples of Scandinavia sometimes referred to the wild and dangerous North Sea as "the cold, gray widow-maker." When life is described as being gray, it has the implication of being austere, harsh, and unfulfilling. However, its neutral stance means that there is hope—after all, it is equally easy for gray to tip in the direction of white as it is to incline toward black. In ancient Jewish mysticism, gray is symbolic of imperturbable wisdom, while to the medieval Church, the color represented humility and penitence and was thus the most commonly used color for monkish habits.

● *Gray is associated with fog and mists.*

Symbolism

The color (or noncolor) gray can be regarded as a messenger; it has commonly been used to represent the more uncanny and mystical aspects of existence. Reports of ghosts and astral visitations are often described as being gray. In keeping with its ghostly symbolism, gray is also the color of mystery, being reminiscent of mists and fog,

Keywords for Gray

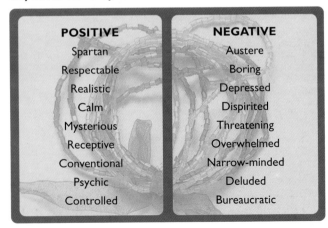

POSITIVE	NEGATIVE
Spartan	Austere
Respectable	Boring
Realistic	Depressed
Calm	Dispirited
Mysterious	Threatening
Receptive	Overwhelmed
Conventional	Narrow-minded
Psychic	Deluded
Controlled	Bureaucratic

Astrology

Being the in-between color, gray is associated with that most ambiguous of planets, Mercury. In Roman mythology, Mercury was more than the messenger of the gods, transmitting information from heaven to Earth and back again. He was also the guide of the dead to the underworld. Mercury was a god whose name became synonymous with deception, with being neither one nor the other (hence his association with gray). The star signs ruled by Mercury are Gemini and Virgo, although I think that we all have an element of a mercurial nature somewhere within us. Mercury is also the planet of the mind.

Feng Shui

Gray has no symbolic direction or connecting animal in the Feng Shui system, although it does have a place as part of the creation cycle of the elements. According to this cycle, fire creates earth in the form of ash. This means that the transforming power of fire consumes its fuel to engender a substance that is receptive to the creation of new life. In other words, gray is representative of the force that replaces the old and makes way for renewal. There is another, more negative, snippet of Feng Shui color theory applicable to this neutral tone: it is said that if a person is continually surrounded by gray, then poverty and suffering will soon follow.

● *Gray can be considered a neutral color, but different textures can raise it above dullness.*

● *Fire creates earth, consuming it as fuel. Gray can represent the ash and smoke.*

The Psychology of Gray

Hard times are indicated when someone habitually wears, or is continually surrounded by, the neutrality of gray. It may be that this person has been overwhelmed by the demands of the outside world and desperately needs calm to recover. These traits can become extreme because an overemphasis on gray can be an indication of depression or even a nervous breakdown. Although the color is not generally used in chromatic healing, light gray is said to stabilize the personality and to be helpful in restoring sane attitudes. Slate gray is particularly symbolic of poverty and austerity, while mid-tone grays represent humility and may, in some cases, indicate a lack of self-esteem and an inability to forgive oneself for past errors. Another, more positive, interpretation of the significance of the color is that it provides the final chance to put right a bad decision.

● *Gray hair is symbolic of wisdom.*

Gray and the Body

Gray is not specifically linked with any bodily parts, although a gray tinge to the skin or the nails is said to indicate congestion somewhere within the body. People with noticeably gray eyes are said to possess a remarkably cool and perceptive character. Gray hair is comfortingly symbolic of wisdom and maturity.

Gray in the Aura

In auric terms, gray is not considered a true color indicative of a character trait. However, a gray hue in any part of the aura, or a grayish tinge to any other color, may show a certain world-weariness or exhaustion.

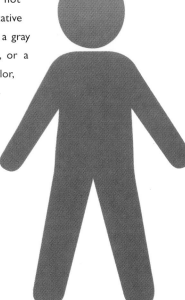

Figures of Speech

Gray has occurred in commonly used expressions throughout the ages. To say that one is "as gray as a badger," or "as a goose," generally means that one is getting on in years. "A Gray Eminence" means the power behind the throne—the phrase is possibly derived from a certain Père Joseph (1577–1638), a Capuchin monk who had a shadowy influence over the policies of Cardinal Richelieu. "Gray matter" is a description of the brain, and, by extension, the mental faculties, the powers of logic, and common sense. "The gray market" was a phrase used during the Second World War to describe a slight breach of rationing regulations that wasn't illegal enough to be considered part of the "black market."

● *Gray is often the color of monks' robes.*

Black and White

It is difficult to consider black and white as individual colors because their symbolism is so intertwined. It is equally difficult to understand these polar opposites except in reference to each other. In short, white is everything that black is not, and vice versa.

● *The symbolism of black and white is often intertwined.*

The most familiar symbol associated with black and white is the *Tai Chi*, or yin-yang symbol of ancient China. In this circular form, black represents the cold, passive, dark, and feminine yin, while white stands for the hot, active, light, and masculine yang. In Western terms, neither black nor white has any astrological symbolism other than standing for night and day.

The Use of Black and White in Decor

In decorative terms, black and white are known as noncolors. They combine to create the most striking, contrasting partnership. This eye-catching partnership has been used again and again throughout decorative history, within designs of fabrics, wall coverings, and all manner of decorative products.

Black and white can be combined with all of the colors of the color wheel to enable the

● *Black and white have been a popular combination in decoration and design for many years.*

decorator or designer to create a wide spectrum of colors. Black added to a color will create a "shade" of the original color; white added creates a "tint"; while the addition of black and white will create a "tone." This is where the saying "to tone it down" originates. By adding black and white, or gray, to a color, it becomes dulled down and loses a great deal of its original strength.

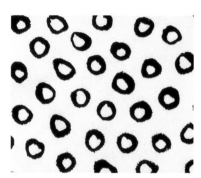

● *Decorating in black and white can achieve a striking effect.*

A room decorated purely in black and white can be very striking. However, it can also appear hard and uncomfortable and should therefore be limited to rooms that rely on impact for their success.

● *Too much black and white together can be very heavy.*

● *Silver and glass can add glamorous accents to a black-and-white scheme.*

Black and white, with the addition of gray or silver, can offer a very successful and more forgiving color combination. This is associated with the art-deco-style interiors of the 1930s, a style that combined geometric-based designs and patterns within a framework of these

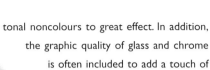
tonal noncolours to great effect. In addition, the graphic quality of glass and chrome is often included to add a touch of glamour to the style.

A more general approach to black and white introduces them to additional colors. For instance, neoclassical interiors combined vivid yellow, black, and white to great effect. The depth of the yellow chosen benefits from the total contrast offered by black-and-white combinations to the scheme. Ceramic flooring in strong, geometric designs in black and white, for example, combine here with classical motifs, such as the urn or scroll. When displayed against a strong, yellow backdrop, this creates a stylish and impressive interior style.

The Victorians also loved the use of geometric designs featuring black and white. Their eclectic style often featured such elements as black-and-white flooring and ceramic tiles.

The introduction of white into a scheme will add a crisp edge to a color selection. White used with cream, for example, will result in the cream looking richer and the white looking brighter. The contrast that white offers to other colors will effectively emphasize the character and intensify the depth of the chosen color.

White reflects light, making it appear farther away. This is why rooms decorated in tints of a color (colors with white added) will always look more spacious than those in darker shades of the same color. White reflects light, whereas black absorbs it, therefore having the opposite effect on a color, and on the illusion of space.

● *Black and white combined with neutral shades and materials can have a relaxing, modern effect.*

Black can add a defining addition to a room: use it to underline or highlight certain features, making them stand out against a colorful or patterned background. Black can also be used to define a space or shape within a room.

The resulting tonal value achieved from the adding of black and white to a color can be used very effectively to alter the perceived appearance of a badly shaped room. This is one of the most useful tools available to the interior designer. By understanding the effects of tone on a space, you can literally transform its appearance.

● *White cabbage rose.*

Chapter 6 The Colors of Gems and Metals

No book on color would be complete without at least a mention of gemstones and metals. From ancient times, each gem has been regarded as a physical expression of color. These gems and metals have taken on the attributes of their color and were often used as amulets and talismans to ward off evil or to attract good health and fortune.

Gems

Amethyst

From Pale Lilac Through Mauve to Purple

Amethyst is a variety of quartz that strengthens endocrine and immune systems. It is said to enhance right-brain activity and to stimulate the pineal and pituitary glands. Amethyst energizes the body and helps to cleanse the blood. It also helps to reduce mental disorders, enabling one to separate reality from illusion. It assists one to overcome baser emotions and to develop one's higher potentials; it is especially useful for those who want to become clairvoyant or psychic. This stone is associated with healing, divine love, inspiration, and intuition, and it is said to work through the third-eye and crown chakras.

Lapis Lazuli

Dark Blue

This is said to strengthen bones, energize the thyroid gland, and release tension and anxiety. It enhances strength, vitality, and energy, but it also opens the psychic centers and enables you to communicate with your higher consciousness. It works through the third-eye and throat chakras.

Sapphire

Blue

Sapphire is said to strengthen the heart and kidneys and to activate the pituitary gland. It stimulates psychic talents and aids clear thinking and inspiration. It encourages creativity, loyalty, and love, and dispels confusion; it is also an excellent aid to meditation. Sapphire works through the third-eye and throat chakras.

Turquoise

Turquoise

This is said to tone and strengthen the body, to aid tissue regeneration, and to improve blood circulation. It is said to help to strengthen the lungs and respiratory system. Turquoise improves meditation and encourages peace of mind and emotional balance. It is also said to bring friendship and loyalty. It works through the throat chakra.

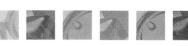

Aquamarine
Blue-green

This African stone is a variety of beryl. It is said to calm the nerves and strengthen the inner organs, such as the liver, spleen, and thyroid gland. It supposedly reduces fluid retention in the body. Aquamarine enhances creativity; on a mental level, it banishes fears and phobias and calms and balances the mind. It is said to enhance inspiration, peace, calmness, and love. It works through the throat and solar-plexus chakras.

Agate
Pale Green to Pale Blue

Agate is a variety of chalcedony and it comes in many colors, but the pale-green or blue varieties are said to tone and strengthen the body and mind and to impart strength and courage. Wearing agate enables you to see through to the truth of a situation and also to accept whatever circumstances you find yourself in. It is considered to be an energetic and powerful healer. Agate works through the heart chakra.

● *Blue lace agate.*

Emerald
Green

The emerald is a variety of beryl and it is more valuable than diamonds. This stone is said to strengthen the heart, liver, kidneys, immune system, and nervous system and to act as a tonic. It enhances one's dreams and is an aid to meditation and spiritual insight. It encourages love, kindness, balance, healing, and patience and works through the heart and solar-plexus chakras.

Citrine
Yellow

Citrine is a variety of quartz that is said to be excellent for the kidneys, colon, liver, gallbladder, digestive organs, and the heart. It removes toxins from the physical, emotional, and mental body and enhances the body's ability to heal itself. Citrine is said to reduce self-destructive tendencies, to raise self-esteem, and to encourage a cheerful outlook, hope, and a light heart. It is also said to encourage money, goods, and plenty. This warming and energizing stone works through the navel and crown chakras.

Amber
Yellow or Brown

Amber is not a stone, but a fossilized resin from prehistoric pine trees. It is said to exert a positive influence on the endocrine system, spleen, and heart by healing, soothing, and harmonizing. It enhances idealism and the ability to do, or to give, without expecting anything in return; it is also claimed to help a person to create a link to their spiritual guides. Amber works through the navel, solar-plexus, and crown chakras.

Carnelian
Orange

Carnelian is a variety of chalcedony and it is said to be an excellent healer that improves the flow of blood around the body. It aids the kidneys, lungs, liver, gallbladder, and pancreas and helps with tissue regeneration. Carnelian enlivens the physical, emotional, and mental parts of the brain and aligns the physical and etheric (or spiritual) bodies. It allows understanding of the inner self and it is an aid to concentration. The heart-warming, joyful, and sociable energies of this stone open the heart to love. Carnelian works through the navel, solar-plexus, and heart chakras.

Jasper
Orange-red

Jasper is a variety of chalcedony. This is said to strengthen the liver, gallbladder, and bladder and it is considered to be a powerful healing stone with a strong impact on the physical body. It works with the lower two chakras.

Garnet
Dark Red

Garnet is said to strengthen and purify, vitalize, and regenerate the body and bloodstream and to stimulate the pituitary gland. It brings love and compassion and enhances the imagination. Garnet works through the base chakra.

Chapter 6 The Colors of Gems and Metals

Ruby
Red

The ruby is said to aid the heart and circulation and to vitalize one's whole system. It stimulates brain functions and eases depression, while encouraging inspiration. This powerful stone enhances clairvoyance and cuts through layers of negativity to bring a person closer to their higher self and spirit guides. It is a very powerful healer that works through all of the chakras.

Other Colors

Diamond
White

Diamonds can be found in several colors, but the most commonly seen are white. This stone is believed to improve the functioning of the brain and to align the cranial bones. It is a great healer that dispels negative thoughts and is said to enhance every part of the mind, body, and spirit. It represents innocence, purity, and faithfulness and is believed to encourage money and goods to come into one's life. White diamond works through all of the chakras.

Moonstone
White

This is said to heal stomach ailments and to improve the spleen, the pancreas, and the pituitary gland. It clears the lymphatic system and relieves anxiety and stress. It is said to aid female ailments and to help during childbirth. The moonstone is believed to enable one to stay on an emotional even keel, to prevent overreaction, and to keep a flexible attitude. It works through the heart chakra.

Obsidian
Black

Obsidian is said to improve the workings of the stomach and intestines, as well as to connect the mind and emotions. It absorbs negativity and reduces stress, while helping to clear unconscious blockages. It enables one to sit quietly and not to be afraid of silence or of being alone; to be detached, at the same time as being wise and loving. It works through the base chakra.

Onyx
Black

Onyx is a variety of chalcedony and it comes in a variety of colors; black onyx is said to balance male and female polarities and to strengthen the bone marrow. It helps one to become more detached and to achieve balance and self-control. Onyx aids inspiration and creativity. Black onyx works with the base chakra.

Rose Quartz
Pink

This is said to aid the kidneys and circulation, to increase fertility, and to ease sexual or emotional imbalances. It helps to clear negative emotions, such as stored anger and resentment, guilt, fear, and jealousy, and it reduces stress, tension, and hot temper. It builds self-confidence and creativity and aids such matters as forgiveness, compassion, and love. Rose quartz works through the heart chakra.

Metals

Copper

Copper is said to influence the flow of blood, to supply energy, and to raise self-esteem. It helps to eliminate toxins and to align the physical and emotional aspects of the body. It aids in recovery from exhaustion and in improving sexual performance. This strong conductor of energy is believed to help those who suffer from rheumatism. It brings a strengthening and masculine energy.

Gold

Gold is said to purify the physical body, to improve circulation, and to strengthen the nervous system. It balances the hemispheres of the brain and aids tissue regeneration. Gold attracts positive energy into the aura and is an aid to clear or inspired thinking. It works through the navel, heart, and crown chakras.

Silver

This is said to enhance the mental functions, to aid circulation, and to strengthen the blood, the pineal gland, and the pituitary glands. It is a stress-reliever that brings emotional balance and helps to improve communication abilities. Silver brings a softening and feminine touch.

Index

Index

Acknowledgments

Bibliography

Colour Healing	Vivian Verner-Bonds	Hermes House	2000
Auras	Sarah Bartlett	Collins and Brown	2000
Feng Shui From Scratch	Jonathan Dee	D&S	2000
Dictionary of Phrase and Fable		Wordsworth	1995
Sun Signs	Sasha Fenton	Thorsons	1992
An Illustrated Encyclopaedia of Traditional Symbols		J.C. Cooper	1978

Credits

Images pp. 6bl, 6tr, 7tl, 7tr, 7br, 8tl, 8bl, 9bl, 9br, 10, 12bl, 12r, 13cl, 13bl, 13tr, 14cl, 14br, 15tr, 15cr, 16t, 31c, 36tr, 42tl, 43t, 46bl, 46tr, 47bl, 47tr, 52bl, 59bl, 59tr, 70bl, 71cl, 75t, 80tr, 80b, 82tl, 91bl, 93tr, 98bl, 98tr, 99bl, 100tl, 100br © Stockbyte

Illustrations pp. 18–19, 47cb by Pauline Cherrett

Angel painting p. 90 by Peter Mallison

(where t = top, b = bottom, l = left, r = right, c = center)